vogue women

georgina howell

PAVILION

First published in Great Britain in 2000 by
PAVILION BOOKS

A member of Chrysalis Books plc

64 Brewery Road, London, N7 9NT

This paperback edition published in 2002
by Pavilion Books

page 1:
Supermodels
Peter Lindbergh, 1990
page 2:
Ines de la Fressange
Albert Watson, 1985

Designed by Mark Thomson, International Design UK Ltd.

A CIP catalogue record for this book is avilaable from the British Library.

ISBN: 1 86205 557 2

Set in **FFScala** and FFScalaSans
Printed in Italy by Conti Tipocolor
Origination by Alliance Graphics, Bedford and Singapore

10 9 8 7 6 5 4 3 2 1

This book can be ordered direct from the publisher.
Please contact the Marketing Department.
But try your bookshop first.

introduction

Distinguished or notorious, pretty or striking, and sometimes all four, the women selected by Vogue over almost a century have a double significance. Photographed by the greatest photographers as the essence of each decade, the ongoing gallery of their spectacular images reveals to us our own aspirations and the changing place of women.

This book follows the Svengali-like influence of the media over raw human material, as each technological advance conjured up the most seductive and appropriate form of beauty for the decade. Newsprint brought us Queen Alexandra's gentle profile, in a glittering tiara. The early fashion magazines familiarized us with duchesses in fancy dress, and musical comedy stars in frocks from the new collections. We came to recognize the faces from the royal enclosure, their patrician features shadowed by their Ascot hats. We backed debutantes like racehorses, tolerant of their high jinks, and tried to predict the winners who would carry off the titles and the money.

Our widening appreciation of individual looks and styles opened out our style horizons. The exotic black dancer Josephine Baker and the Gothic eccentric Edith Sitwell prepared us in the 1920s for the chic fashion monkeys of the 1930s – Baba d'Erlanger who, as

Audrey Hepburn
Cecil Beaton, 1964

a child, had a turbanned mameluke instead of a nanny, and Coco Chanel, who wore men's clothes. When the movies first allowed us to see women feeling and thinking just like us, we gazed at the new array of beauties on offer and became type-conscious for the first time. A new link was made between fan and idol – were we the Dietrich or the Clara Bow type?

Wartime took away the fun and brought us back to a heroic sentimentality. Every Englishwoman was a sensible English rose buckling to, doing her bit. Even high society had to be seen to dig lettuces, or smooth a pillow. In the black and white pages of our reduced magazines the classic beauty returned to us in the form of Lady Diana Cooper, in a headscarf, feeding the pigs.

When the tide of war passes, we escape into other realities. While governments coerce us into drab economies, films and couture conspire to meet our appetites for visions of exotic beauty and extreme fashion. Even Princess Margaret wore the New Look: in her racy prime, she was ready to jump on a motorbike or camp it up by the piano.

Glamour was reborn in Paris, and models became interesting. The first models had been anonymous skivvies, sewing on buttons and delivering parcels between trying on outfits. Now, as Living Inspirations, they acquired status and were permitted a Christian name. Balenciaga had Ali, Christian Dior had Lucky, Yves had Victoire. The upwardly mobile models who followed were promoted to the dignity of a surname. Vogue drew attention to such stylish beauties as Marie-Hélène Arnaud and Suzy Parker, and hinted at their backstage power. These house models prefigured the muses and stylists of the 1980s and 90s – Inès de la Fressange, Loulou de la Falaise and Amanda Harlech. By doing their thing, by representing and updating the ever-ageing couturiers, they have been able to earn as much as heads of industry.

As in the 1957 Audrey Hepburn/Fred Astaire movie Funny Face, styled by the great fashion photographer Richard Avedon, the top photographers and fashion editors were able, by devoting their talents to one star model, to create a fashion icon. In the world of the photographic model, Barbara Goalen and Fiona Campbell Walter were the forerunners of the supermodels who followed in the late 1980s. When David Bailey recorded his obsession with Jean Shrimpton on the pages of Vogue, he introduced sex into the fashion equation for the first time. The age of models dropped to 18, or even 16 and 14. Models no longer stood in unnatural attitudes in front of Georgian houses, staring haughtily into the distance. They sprawled, clambered over cars, sucked their thumbs, ran from helicopters or confronted the lens with an uncompromising stare. Vogue models became pin-ups in prisons and garages.

Bailey had captured the attention of the young, and brought fashion closer to life, just as the stylist-photographers of the 1980s and 90s made Vogue relevant to teenage MTV audiences.

The book scrutinizes beauty that survives radical changes in taste and fashion. What fairy godmother blessed Lady Diana Cooper with looks that lasted from 1920 to 1980? How did (now Dame) Elizabeth Taylor remain a star for 30 years, from the vulnerable 14 year old of National Velvet to the raucous matriarch of Who's Afraid of Virginia Woolf? in which she starred with Richard Burton? Is beauty a genetic phenomenon, passing predictably down the line, as it appears to have done in the great female dynasties of the Falaises, the Redgraves and the Frasers? Or is it that each generation rises to the occasion, recognizing and honoring the family precedent?

The Vogue 'treatment' has always included portraiture by the great photographers. The great in-house expertise has also provided tweaking in the make-up and hair department, and the head-to-toe editing that sent the late Princess of Wales running up the back stairs of the Hanover Square office in the early years of her marriage.

Make-up and good lighting can do much for a woman, but cannot explain the full metamorphosis from underwhelming to unforgettable. 'Before' and 'After' photographs of a woman who becomes world-famous show us two incarnations of the same features and personality – we ask: Before and After what? Here is Jackie Kennedy as a beetle-browed teenager with an unnaturally broad face. Here is Jackie Kennedy as the ravishingly modern, adorably immaculate First Lady, as her husband, the President, tells the Assembly 'I have come to Paris to accompany my wife.' Is there a mechanism that acts like a trigger to beauty, and do we all have that mental or biological switch, ready to be turned on and off?

Glamour runs like mercury from profession to profession. The chronology of female popular aspiration passes from ballerinas and air hostesses to actresses and journalists, aid workers and singers. As movie stars sought gravitas in the late 1980s through 5000-word newspaper and magazine profiles, they retreated from the fashion pages. Ballerinas declined to be used as clothes horses. Models took up center stage again in the form of the long-lived supermodels, trophies to be hunted by cosmetic companies and fashion magazines. These were the women whose agents fought for buy-out exclusive contracts, the girls who 'wouldn't get out of bed for less than $20,000'.

The music industry waifs produced their own wrecked type of beauty in a druggy subtext to the alienating, wholesome glamour of the supermodels. At the same time the society women we admired at the beginning of the century have returned to us in vigorous

Diana
Patrick Demarchelier, 1994

new forms, as the hautbo heiresses, the fashion eccentrics and the busy small-change personalities of the gossip columns. Magazines have sprung up to chronicle the calendar-perfect lives and shadowless faces of the famous-for-being-famous.

Rising supreme, Princess Diana was the single most admired blonde of the century, whose death at the height of her beauty has, like Marilyn Monroe's, enshrined her as something more than an idol, an icon.

We know what happened to Diana and to Monroe. What became of the other women we wanted to look like, and how were they treated? Happy endings have been few and far between, with alcoholism, drug addiction and breakdowns unusually common. Bronwen Pugh became Lady Astor and retreated for the rest of her life into a mysterious rural commune. Grace Kelly married a prince but sublimated her feelings of futility in devotion to a dangerous religious sect. Sally Croker Poole married the Aga Khan, and divorced with evident relief. Fiona Campbell Walter married Baron von Thyssen, and immediately sued for divorce. Marie Helvin is now single again and Jerry Hall has consulted her lawyer.

We opened the century wanting to look like aristocrats or actresses, and ended it wanting to look like television presenters and the wives of football stars. Over the years we have plucked our eyebrows to be like Garbo and shaved our heads to look like Annie Lennox. We have gone bouffant with Elizabeth Taylor and Egyptian with Penelope Tree. In the name of beauty, we have tried white lipstick and green nails and studs in our tongues and navels. The next transformations may come from the stars of virtual reality or three-dimensional holograms, or even from the brutalism of total visual access, bedroom to bedroom via the Web. Then beauty will truly be in the eye of the beholder.

If we place classical beauties in a central vertical band, from Gladys Cooper to Grace Kelly and Sharon Stone, with pretty, fluffy women to the left and jolie-laides to the right, then the pendulum of fashion has gradually swung from left to right. As the media has brought its subjects closer, and presented them to us more insistently, we have learned to appreciate female beauty in all its color and variety. Today, a woman is not disqualified from beauty because she has a large bony nose, like Barbra Streisand's, or by the color of her skin, like Iman or Naomi Campbell, or because of oversized features, like Julia Roberts's, or an albino angularity, like the late Carolyn Bessette Kennedy's. Margaux Hemingway became a movie star without plucking her eyebrows and Lauren Hutton became the best-paid model of the decade without getting rid of the gap between her front teeth. All have a place in the gallery of 20th-century beauty.

1 *royalty*

It would have been wonderful for Vogue if all the royal women had been beauties, or even fashionable. Instead, Queen Mary, the wife of George v, maintained an unsmiling headmistressy profile on the throne for the first 20 years of British Vogue's life.

The world's best secret trade magazine, Vogue's job was, is and will be to help sell fashion, and to do it without a hint of vulgar commerce. The success of the magazine has always been due to its talent for inducing aspiration. It doesn't just report fashion or create fashion. It bridges the gap between the reader and the frock by its discriminating choice of the women shown on the fashion and feature pages. It is the Vogue woman who 'sells' the clothes to the readers.

The editors could pick and choose from the ranks of society girls and models; they could make over a sportswoman or the plain daughter of a duchess; they could put a musical comedy actress in a couture ballgown; but they were stuck with royalty. With few exceptions, the princesses and queens of Britain were impervious to fashion and therefore quite useless to Vogue. Their own adornment symbolized social and cultural stability, continuity and changelessness, while the definition of fashion is change.

Already forgotten was the arrogant glamour of the Winterhalter beauties of the high Victorian era: Princess Metternich in her Worth ballgown of silver lamé with scarlet daisies, or Elizabeth of Austria in her veiled topper and green velvet riding habit, the train flying after her as she cleared hedge after hedge on the hunting field. How those first Vogue editors must have wished that Alexandra was still Queen, instead of being the dowager. The daughter of Christian xi of Denmark, married to Edward vii in 1863, she was ineffably chic. She had a slender, hourglass figure and wore tailored embroidered costumes, the jackets tightly belted over great, swaying crinolines. After the death of Edward, she wore coatees over the crinolines, little high-necked jackets embroidered with sequins. Her hair was curled and pinned high on her head, the tiny beribboned bowler that became her trademark tipped over her large grey eyes. With her gentle manners and her slight Danish accent, she delighted everyone she met: from an evening in her company admirers would take away impressions of a charming and feminine woman – the glitter of a tiara, candlelight on lace.

By contrast, Princess Mary of Teck was a strong, dutiful woman. When her first choice of a fiancé, the Prince of Wales, died in 1892, she switched her affections without apparent difficulty to marry his younger brother, who became the conscientious George v. Early in her life Queen Mary became a patrician figure in a toque massed with parma violets, with fabulous diamonds at her throat. Her prow-like bosom dangled a lorgnette among the

Queen Mary
Bassano

chinchillas. She never dressed fashionably, of course – she knew it was not part of her remit – but a consistency of taste led at least to a recognizable style. She was dignified, if stiff, and in genteel aristocratic England she was not without her admirers.

In her day, wealthy, aristocratic women considered high fashion as vulgar and exhibitionistic. When researching the turn of the century for his exhibition of society fashion at the Victoria & Albert at the end of 1971, Cecil Beaton discovered that women from distinguished families in Italy and Argentina had 'rested' boxes of new Paris couture clothes in the attic for six months or more, until the dresses had become less startlingly fashionable.

These attitudes were a legacy of the mores of turn-of-the-century Paris, where the 'grand horizontals', the cocottes and mistresses of the wealthy, were given spectacular clothing free of charge by the couture houses on account of the women's beauty and high visibility. A modern comparison might be the Versace dresses worn by Elizabeth Hurley to movie premieres. Many English and Scottish women who could have afforded Bond Street or the rue Faubourg preferred to go to the village seamstress, just as elderly dukes tended to go about in older clothes than their chauffeurs or gardeners.

Elizabeth Bowes-Lyon, the fiancée of the future George VI, was a welcome contrast to Queen Mary. She had china-blue eyes and a warm personality, but she came from a plain-living happy family from Scotland, the Strathmores, and was far too well brought up to be fashionable. She had made her own clothes since the schoolroom. Entering public life when cinema and the popular picture press were just starting to come into their own, it was easy to see that she was no sophisticated fashion plate. The then Mrs Winston Churchill described her as 'very sweet and soignée like a plump turtle dove'. It was Norman Hartnell who discovered the way to make the most of her picturesque and romantic appearance in evening dress. Inspired by the Winterhalter portraits he saw in the state apartments of Buckingham Palace, he dressed her in puff sleeves and tucked bodices, demure necklines and colors that 'carried' to the crowd. Afternoon hats rolled back from the candid brow, tulle sparkled, fabric flowers were pinned among the sapphires and diamonds.

Elizabeth Bowes-Lyon
Van Dyke, 1919

HM Queen Elizabeth
Cecil Beaton, 1939

The greatest fashion triumph of her career was the wardrobe Hartnell made for her state visit to Paris in the summer of 1938. Almost as the visit was due to begin, her mother, Lady Strathmore, died. Hartnell had already completed some 30 grand dresses plus coats and accessories in a range of colors. Now it was remembered that Queen Victoria had insisted on a white funeral, and that white could be the color of royal mourning. The trip to Paris was set back a few weeks so that the clothes could be remade, and the Bruton Street salon worked around the clock to reproduce each garment in white.

The Parisians, the cruellest sartorial critics on earth, had openly mocked Queen Victoria on her state visit for her dusty travelling bonnet and handbag crudely embroidered with a comic poodle. They wondered what the new Queen would wear, anticipated disaster, and were swept off their feet by Elizabeth's freshness and charm, her blue eyes and perfect skin, and the starry appeal of her filmy white dresses and parasols. When she appeared at a garden party at the Bagatelle, face framed against a snowy parasol, her lace dress trailing behind her across the grass, she won all hearts. The tour to the USA the following spring echoed her success in Paris. It was the year of Gone with the Wind. The crinolines and parasols went straight into the fashion vocabulary of Fifth Avenue, already saturated with Victorian nostalgia. For the first time in a hundred years, albeit by accident, royalty had set fashion. The whole of America was star-struck for Vivien Leigh and Elizabeth of England.

Hartnell was less successful in designing the Queen's bread-and-butter daytime wardrobe. His plan was to give the Queen the chic of the top actress on the London stage, Evelyn Laye, but he discovered that the reality fell short of the ideal when the hips were less bony, the ankles less slim. In the end it was the very restrictions of wartime clothing that limited the choice and provided the right formulas. Elizabeth chose to set an example and obey the government rules for 'austerity' dressing. Hartnell pared down the look, and simplified. During the war years, the Queen dressed down and was cheered as she inspected bomb sites in homely serviceable tweeds, the image of a sympathetic wife and mother. Later, she chose to dress up at all times as if it was evening, with the fluttering of pastel crepe and chiffon, the drift of ostrich feathers, the little snub-toed high heeled shoes, the gentle operatic gesture of her hand as she waved to the crowd. It is a look not only loved by the public. French avant-garde couturiers such as Christian Lacroix, Jean Paul Gaultier and Azzadine Alaia today profess themselves passionate fans of her look.

If Elizabeth was Odette, the swan princess in white, then Odile, the bad fairy, was Wallis Simpson, hard and chic in her black Molyneux suits. Wallis openly mocked

Duke of Windsor and Wallis Simpson
Cecil Beaton, 1937

right:
Princess Margaret
Cecil Beaton, 1951

Elizabeth's lack of sophistication and referred to her as 'Cookie', joking that she had a cook's figure and a cook's taste. As the public came to understand the game that Wallis was playing, as she distracted and drew the Prince of Wales away from his royal duties, British taste polarized. Wallis, the bandbox fashion plate, became the most unpopular woman throughout Britain. There was a sense abroad once more that high fashion was the province of the worldly, the irresponsible, and especially the wicked foreigner.

By the time Elizabeth and Margaret had grown up, the press was firmly in the picture, and the royals were on their guard. Elizabeth, a dutiful girl painfully determined to be serious and worthy of the task ahead, seemed never to be out of uniform. The theatrical, beautiful Margaret suffered the fate that had traditionally been meted out to the younger son of the future monarch. If Elizabeth was the heir, Margaret was the spare who recognized she was second best, but still had to maintain the duties and decorous standards expected. She was restricted and yet given identity by her closeness to the throne.

As a young woman she was photographed by Cecil Beaton in acres of white tulle with blossom and mist. Far more interested in fashion than Elizabeth, she tried to emerge from the puff sleeves and twinsets that had been imposed on her since her teens. With her violet eyes and hourglass figure, she was the beauty of the family, and she liked to experiment with fashion. Her flirtations with it mark the happiest, and the most liberated periods of her life. In 1947, she gave her seal of approval to the New Look of Christian Dior – condemned by British officialdom because the feminine curves and romantic flowing lines thwarted fabric restrictions – by wearing it everywhere and persuading the Queen, her mother, to endorse it, too.

When she became the last member of the royal family to make a supreme sacrifice to duty, when she gave up the possibility of marrying the handsome, stammering equerry, Peter Townsend, she seemed to return to the forgettable royal uniform of cardigans and kilts, lumpy tweeds and satin stoles. It was not until she married the photographer Anthony Armstrong-Jones, whose work for Vogue had included fashion shoots, that she blossomed again. Perhaps he 'edited' her for the camera. For a while she abandoned her

Princess Elizabeth and Prince Charles
Cecil Beaton, 1948

favorite scarves and stubby shoes, lost weight and appeared in crisp Jackie Kennedy type coats with pillbox hats and bracelet length sleeves. While the Queen's 'look' was formulated to please the crowd, with necklines designed to focus on her fabulous jewels and colors that would carry across a field, Margaret had a little more freedom, and she used it to wear opaque and colored tights with big fur and feather hats. Sun spectacles and a long cigarette holder became her trademarks.

This was the liberating period during which, on a foreign cruise, she came ashore and stunned the reception committee by jumping on the back of a motorbike driven by Snowdon, and roaring away over the horizon. However, decorum soon reasserted itself.

Her life, never quite fulfilled, has a sadness to it. Brought up to pomp and circumstance and now living quite an ordinary life, she has nevertheless proved to be an excellent mother. Her daughter and son, to date, have made a great success of their lives.

The Greek princess, Marina, became the most elegant royal woman when she married the Duke of Kent in 1934. Brought up in Paris, she was naturally chic and handsome rather than pretty, and had an attractive Greek accent. Her family had been so short of money that she had once posed for an advertisement for Pond's Cold Cream – something that must have shocked the Windsors. She wore 'Marina blue' – a shadowy turquoise – and was usually seen in trimly tailored suits with little hats tipped over her forehead. She gave the new couture house of Captain Molyneux her patronage and he dressed her beautifully in gentle, understated clothes, notably in suits with fur collars. She never adopted the padded shoulders of the 1930s, but originated many fashions of her own, such as the double pearl choker. For evenings in public she wore bias cut satins, and looked as good in them as any of Noël Coward's sophisticated comedy actresses such as Gertrude Lawrence or Adrienne Allen. At George v's Jubilee, she looked ravishing in a huge grey straw hat crowned with ostrich feathers. It was criticized by the press for hiding half her face, and she did not repeat the experiment.

By the time Vogue photographer Norman Parkinson came to take the engagement photographs of Princess Anne in 1973, make-up expertise and camera technology had made it possible virtually to transform the looks of the most reluctant beauty. As ever, the magazine had found photographers of such urbanity and charm that they could persuade even royals to make the necessary effort. Even so, Parkinson had hilarious trouble winning the cooperation of this championship horsewoman. He said afterwards 'The royal family face the camera so often they just want to get it over with. If you meet later, they will ask "Did the

Princess Marina of Kent
Cecil Beaton, 1938

snaps come out?"' After photographing the Princess in one evening dress, Parkinson asked her if she would be kind enough to try on another. 'She came back in double quick time, and I soon saw why. She hadn't bothered to take off the first dress. She had simply put the second one on top of the first!'

His pictures of Anne made her look stunning, if a little unlike herself. But when he suggested putting her on a horse, the resulting joyous picture became possibly the best portrait she will ever have, capturing both her athletic skill and dashing grace.

Almost the entire century passed before a royal woman at last ruffled the surface of fashion. For nearly a hundred years, while the Russian ballet came and went and Josephine Baker brought Africa to Paris; while women in men's clothes broke sporting records; while the movie industry unfolded and women went to work; while men walked on the moon; and while androgyny and fetishism and pornography reached the high street; royalty maintained a studied indifference to the sartorial changes that these events brought.

And then came Diana.

Princess Anne
Norman Parkinson, 1969

right:
Helen Windsor
Snowdon, 1982

2

society girls

When a woman buys a copy of Vogue, she hopes to find the magic ingredient that will enable her to become, in some undefined way, more than she was yesterday. Vogue's inspirational early publisher, Condé Nast, turned the magazine into a machine for supplying this ingredient.

The world beyond, which Vogue purveyed, was the epitome of glamour, wealth and power: in a word, society. As Condé Nast's biographer Caroline Seebohm records, his vision was purely aesthetic. His intention was to produce the most beautiful and tasteful magazine that had ever existed. Vogue would chronicle the élite and everything that composed their style of life, not forgetting their sophisticated appreciation of fashion and art, and deliver it into the hands of the young and hungry country that was America, with all its new wealth and social ambition.

'Does the young woman in Fort Smith, or San Antonio, or Birmingham, or Topeka', asked the New York Herald Tribune in Nast's obituary, 'dress somewhat better than her ancestors, and does she have a surer appreciation of the world of manners and decorum and what might be called the art of gracious living? Then much of the credit must go to Condé Nast.'

Acquiring Vogue in 1909, he was confronted with an apparently insuperable problem. The inherently wealthy and well-born had no need to appear in the magazine. They had more reasons, in fact, to avoid publicizing their exclusive and comfortable lives. What inducements could Vogue offer to entice them into the pages of the magazine? The way to approach them, he soon divined, was from the inside, on their own level. His answer was to give two fabulous parties a month for the 17 years between 1925 and 1942.

At each of these parties, stylistic perfection combined with a scintillating guest list to create social history. Guests were divided into A, B and C groups: society, people in the arts, and celebrities. The glittering stage to which Nast attracted these stars was a penthouse apartment of 30 rooms, its ballroom hung with an 18th-century Chien Lung wallpaper, its conservatory dining room a bower of flowers suspended in the moonlight above the sparkle of Park Avenue. Decorated by the first professional female interior decorator of America, Elsie de Wolfe, enfilades of rooms revealed Louis XV furniture, needlepoint sofas, grisaille walls, silk moiré curtains and Savonnerie rugs. In the hands of the meticulous, shy publisher, party-giving became a precise science. Orchestras and bands were carefully auditioned, thousands of dollars' worth of flowers were trucked in, elevators cleaned and scented, rows of dishwashers installed, armies of waiters inspected for the starchiness of their

Paula Gellibrand
Cecil Beaton, 1928

right:
Lady Honor Channon
Cecil Beaton

shirts and napkins, lighting and ventilation checked, remeasured and checked again.

His parties were virtual fashion parades of the most chic and glamorous women in the world. From the moment one of Nast's thick engraved invitations fell through the letterbox, a guest would begin to plan her outfit with the anxiety of a bride deciding on her wedding dress. She might find herself in competition with Josephine Baker in a bias white dress by Vionnet, with white silk butterflies in her hair, or Tallulah Bankhead in a river of gold sequins, or the Duchess of Windsor in a Mainbocher gown.

It was all, of course, wonderful copy, and most of the guests and the parties would inevitably appear in Vogue in all their sartorial glory, becoming a staple of the American gossip columns. Many of the women, and some of the men, became contributors to the magazine, even figuring on the masthead, for which they received a modest retainer. But no-one monitored the social scene more scrupulously than Nast himself. His staff remembered him cross-examining an editor who had just arrived from Newport, asking 'What were the chauffeurs wearing?'

A single rich woman buying expensive dresses for her friends to admire at discreet parties does nothing to promote the wares of the couturier. Vogue served the fashion industry by making the electric connection. Readers were alerted to the meaning of style, they copied the society stars, the couture name sold the ready-to-wear, fashion changes were copied around the world, advertising revenue burgeoned and the mass market boomed. The engine had roared into life. Vogue has continued to serve its sponsors well in portraying a vigorous society, however that world has changed.

Even the richest of women can be tempted to have her photograph taken if it is by a great photographer. Nast lost no time in finding and winning over great new photographers who guaranteed a flattering and fashionable portrait. These were such masters of the art as Baron de Mayer, master of sparkling light, Steichen or Stieglitz, the brilliant Hoyningen-Huene and Horst, or Cecil Beaton. But the publisher required something more. He wanted portraits that expressed the glamorous world that these women inhabited. It was not enough, for instance, to show Honor Channon, the daughter of Lord Iveagh and the wife

Nancy, Diana, Jessica and Unity Mitford
1932

of social diarist 'Chips' Channon, looking pretty. She was to be photographed in her spectacular blue and silver Belgrave Square dining room, modelled on a famous room in the Amalienburg Palace. Readers could examine the room in which guests such as the Prince of Wales and Mrs Simpson ate off a gold-plated dinner service which had once belonged to Napoleon, and which was said to have cost more than the entire room. Another guest, Harold Nicolson, described the room in a letter to his wife, the great gardener Vita Sackville-West, 'Oh my God how rich and powerful "Lord" Channon has become! The dining room is entered through an orange lobby and discloses itself ... baroque and rococo and what-ho and oh-no-no and all that. Very fine indeed.'

In his own diaries, Chips Channon described his sometime guest Mrs Simpson as 'a jolly unprepossessing American, witty, a mimic, an excellent cook' and noted that she had completely 'subjugated' the Prince of Wales. 'She is madly anxious to storm society while she is still his favorite.'

Not quite a gossip magazine, Vogue found ways to titillate its attentive readers. The Simpson scandal, the greatest drama of the 30s, happened well within Vogue's scope. Mrs Simpson's name first appears in British Vogue in 1935, obliquely mentioned in connection with groups including the Prince of Wales. Readers are informed that for cocktails 'hot sausages ... are out of date, back numbers. You must think up something different. The Prince of Wales has hot buttered American soda biscuits, with cod's roe, served in hot silver breakfast dishes' and, a sentence or two further down the page 'Mrs Simpson's food is of such a high standard that the intelligent guest fasts before going to have cocktails with her ... her hot dishes are famous'. In the copy, the two names were never far apart. 'The Prince of Wales went by boat to dine at St Tropez ... and acquired a blue and white striped sailor's pullover.' In the next column readers learnt that 'The best-dressed women, like Mrs Ernest Simpson, for example, have Schiaparelli's dresses.'

In wartime, by contrast, society women had to be seen as worthy, patriotic figures. During the First World War it became their ambition to be photographed in a ravishing uniform, like Countess Bathurst in her Red Cross outfit, or the Marchioness of Londonderry in the uniform of the Women's Service Legion. The Duchess of Wellington was photographed knitting a sock for a soldier. In the Second World War, Cecil Beaton picked his

Mary Churchill
Cecil Beaton

Margaret, Duchess of Argyll
Robert Haswell, 1962

right:
Alice Ormsby-Gore
David Montgomery, 1969

way carefully through the mud to photograph Churchill's daughter Mary baling up the hay, and Lady Diana Cooper feeding her pigs and chickens.

Women like these were copied, for better or worse. When Margaret Whigham, daughter of a wealthy industrialist and 'Deb of the Year' got married to Charles Sweeny in 1933, thousands turned out on the streets to see her in her dress of ivory satin and seed pearls, with its 28-foot train. A Sunday Graphic reporter wrote 'I discovered in the crowds that fought to see her married, scores of young women who had modelled their appearance on hers with long earrings, cupid bow lips and tiny hats aslant as "the Wigham" wears them.' Said to have been the first debutante to have employed a press agent, she was immortalised in a song by Cole Porter: 'You're the nimble tread of the feet of Fred Astaire, You're Mussolini, You're Mrs Sweeny, You're Camembert ...' Married for the second time, to the Duke of Argyll, she became a notorious figure when he tried to have her banned from his ancestral home, and her scandalous life became public knowledge in the bitter divorce that followed.

Whether it is Queen Charlotte's Ball in the 30s, or the Chelsea Arts Ball in the 60s, or the charity extravaganzas of the White House in the 80s, it is at parties that society is identified and defined for the decade. At the millennium, to quote the Economist magazine, 'Parties are becoming more important than ever. Businesses are increasingly "relationship-driven", dominated by alliances, mergers and teams, while in other social contexts the growth of telecommunications means that people come in contact with a wider variety of people outside of work as well'. According to the anthropologist William Ury, associate director of Harvard Law School's research program on negotiation, the role of parties in supplying a horizontal bridging role, giving people a different context in which to relate, is crucial to society.

Today, an evening such as the one given in 1999 by Versace, De Beers and Krug and put together by public relations diva Aurelia Cecil at London's Syon House, with its Robert Adam interior and 30 acre Capability Brown garden resounding to the music of Bon Jovi, can guarantee $20 million worth of publicity around the world. Just as Condé Nast foresaw at the very start of the century, parties have become very big business.

Tara Palmer-Tomkinson
Neil Kirk, 1997

right:
Jemima Khan
Oberto Gili, 1998

3

inspirations

The minds of Vogue's readers, determined Condé Nast, should be as elegantly dressed as their bodies. It was his ambition that his magazine for the élite should furnish women with the ability to hold up their end of a dinner party conversation, be the subject art, politics, science, entertainment, economics or medical breakthroughs. Features such as 'Is ageing really necessary?', 'Why is Britain in debt?' or 'What changes will the next century bring us?' were sandwiched between 'The waist is back!' and 'Il faut skimp pour être chic'.

Vogue's unique pull with society figures gave it unparalleled access, for any magazine and particularly any woman's magazine, to the important people of the day. The many distinguished contributors and staff members who figured on Vogue's international mastheads over the century brought a larger sense of fashion and style to Vogue's remit. Because of the larger map they drew in its pages, fashion lost its sillier connotations and found its proper place as one of the decorative arts, and part of civilized life.

The fact that the sculptor and photographer Alexander Liberman worked on Vogue from 1941 and became editorial director in chief of all the Vogues ensured that most of the avant-garde artists – albeit the ones he approved – were profiled in the magazines by knowledgeable critics. The arts pages, however, represented just a fraction of those devoted to fashion and beauty, and whenever culture threatened to oust frocks as Vogue's raison d'être, the magazine would lose money. In 1926 Condé Nast reluctantly fired its British Vogue editor Dorothy Todd, a lesbian of literary leanings, under whose management the London office was losing £25,000 a year. Todd had hired such talents as Raymond Mortimer, Alan Pryce-Jones, Peter Quennell, David Garnett and Aldous Huxley. She was the first to show the work of Jean Cocteau in England, and to publish Gertrude Stein's verse, with a commentary by Edith Sitwell. The 20s issues of Vogue remain a wonderfully stimulating documentary of life at the turning point of the century.

Vogue always aimed to be an inspiration, responding to the aspirations of its readers, usually by exhorting them to make the best of themselves. In the early years, and particularly in wartime, this sentiment was aggressively stated, in the manner of a gym mistress instructing schoolgirls to brace up and make an effort. When your soldier came back from the front, said Vogue in the First World War, 'Make it your business to see that he carries away with him on his return to duty a refreshing vision of loveliness, and in particular to avoid the masculine.' For most of the Second World War, the editorials adhered to Ministry of Information propaganda. After all, the main source of wartime revenue were the advertisements placed by the Ministries of Fuel and Power, Food and Health. Readers were

Colette
c. 1920

right:
Nancy Astor
1920

told that they need not fear rationing and clothes coupons because 'Your wardrobe, instead of being a three-volume novel, will now be a short story in which every line will count. You want to look as if you cared about your looks, but cared more about being able to do a full day's work'.

Towards VE day, Vogue began to acquire a distinctly subversive and independent tone of voice which was quite new: 'It is unfair and economically unwise', it said, 'to leave our designers, one moment longer than necessary, at such a disadvantage in relation to our competitors.' The magazine was responding to the readers' exasperation with austerity. Women were prepared to make huge sacrifices for the war effort, but after six years, and with peace in view, they expected some let-up. And for the first time in the pages of Vogue, a woman let fly. Marghanita Laski wrote 'Patriotism is NOT ENOUGH, and I, for one, am fed up. I'm fed up at home, and I'm fed up when I go abroad. I don't like to see the foreigner pointing and whispering "You can see she's English – look at her clothes".' The instant adoption of Christian Dior's New Look in 1947, in the teeth of government opposition, was Vogue's first, and perhaps only, inspiring victory.

Ground-breaking social change did not fall into Vogue territory. It wasn't that kind of magazine, and if it had been, it would not have been so successful. What it could do, and do brilliantly, was to produce great photographs of the inspirational figures of the day, even if they were published in gallery sections without much comment, and for the sole reason that the names were au courant. 'People are Talking About ...' was one of Vogue's longest running features. The really distinguished were present in force – from Mrs Thatcher to Mother Teresa – but often the frivolous personalities were the most entertaining. Inconsequential as they may have been, they were a pleasing addition to the features pages and conveyed the new directions that readers might take. In Vogue in the 20s and 30s you were able to see explorers such as Madame Corniglion, in a pith helmet, hitching up her skirt to wade through a tributary of the Niger, while her Rolls Royce was rafted across beside her, shepherded by a team of locals, or Mrs Vanderbilt 'keeping cool in darkest Africa in a Patou dress'.

There were sportswomen such as Suzanne Lenglen, sailing across the tennis court, using her racquet like a ladle, in the short pleated dress with which she revolutionized tennis wear. Her arrival on court, to rapturous applause, was something to see.

Suzanne Lenglen
1922

right:
Coco Chanel
Cecil Beaton, 1936

following pages, left:
Rebecca West
Cecil Beaton, 1942
following pages, right:
Lee Miller
Clifford Coffin

She always wore a chic white bandeau, and arrived in a white cashmere coat by Patou, carrying an enormous bouquet of white flowers.

There were portraits of American ace airwoman of the 40s, Jacqueline Cochran, holder of 17 air speed records, elegant in sun spectacles and a crisp white shirt, leaning negligently against the propeller of her plane, and of Nancy Astor, the first woman MP to take her seat in the House of Commons. It was Nancy Astor who provoked a famous Churchill witticism when he met her in the corridors of Westminster. 'Winston – you're drunk! Horribly drunk!' Nancy Astor exclaimed. 'Madam, you are ugly – horribly ugly!' he responded. 'But I shall be sober in the morning.'

The outspoken Margot Asquith, Lady Oxford, wife of the former Liberal Prime Minister, contributed several articles to Vogue. The story went that when she was introduced to the famous film actress Jean Harlow, the star said 'Pleased to meet you, Margot', sounding the T. Asquith icily responded 'The T is silent, as in Harlow.'

In the 30s, when open-air living and the example of the movie stars had made women body-conscious, slimming led to obsessive dieting and Vogue beauty articles majored on the craze. Mrs Syrie Maugham, the decorator famous for her 'all-white' rooms, was one such. 'Went to the first of Mrs Maugham's diet lunch parties', wrote the Voguette from the features department. 'She decided to devote the first quiet spell to the interests of health and made it known to her friends that any who were feeling the effects of overeating and a long siege of strenuous partying could come any day to lunch or dine with her on regime food.' Mrs Maugham finally went on the diet of diets, and told Vogue, 'I starved for 6 weeks. Yes, literally, for 6 weeks I ate nothing at all ... yet I never missed a day's work, and feel better than I can ever remember.' Even if Vogue has counselled the reader on losing weight for the last 80 years, it has not neglected the art of producing delicious food. It also published a rare early interview with the food scholar and perfectionist Elizabeth David, who raised cookery writing to the level of literature.

Then there were Vogue's own editors, the incisive, elegant and somewhat haughty women to whom style was oxygen: Patricia Cunningham, married to English couturier Charles Creed, and Lady Rendlesham, whose Young Idea began as a device to turn 60s teenagers into Vogue readers, and ended by influencing the entire magazine. There was Grace Coddington, who was able to change her look completely from time to time, as fashion

Daphne du Maurier
Clifford Coffin, 1946

dictated. In all her manifestations, she exerted a considerable influence on the style of the 70s through designers, who liked her to wear their clothes, on photographers, who liked to photograph her, and on models and readers, who have copied her.

From the 50s onwards, the subject of women and careers was up for discussion. Writing about the work of Frances Hodgkins, the painter, who died in 1947, Myfanwy Evans said: 'Many women who are creative artists of any kind manage to achieve their work in spite of the fact that they also live normal (if nerve-wracked) lives as women, with husband, home, children, clothes, servants and so on; it is the intensity with which they can withdraw from the world at the time that they are working that makes them into amateurs or professionals; the degree to which they can bear to be so much in the wrong as to be thoroughly selfish, at times, that makes them good or indifferent artists ... a few take the most difficult way, and, remaining solitary, live or die by their work. Frances Hodgkins was one of these.'

It was no longer bad form to be 'unfeminine'. Daphne du Maurier, the novelist, took up the cudgels in 1946. 'I am composing a letter to The Times, never published, on the subject of birth control. The birthrate is falling, and I know why, and so do all the other women of my generation. It has nothing to do with insecurity or atom-bombs or the movies. It is because we don't want a lot of children, and had the women of past generations known how to limit their families they would have done so.'

The groundswell grew. Germaine Greer, whose intelligent book The Female Eunuch gave rise to a great deal of journalistic debate and dinner-party bickering in the 70s, was interviewed for Vogue by Kathleen Tynan. The book had just come out in the USA with a first printing of 75,000 copies, and serialization in three leading American magazines. Greer's argument was that women do not suffer from penis envy as Freud taught, but from the castration and distortion of the natural female personality. Tynan found her 'boldly dressed and bra-less, with a long Pre-Raphaelite face, and a voice that can be stridently vulgar ... funny, outrageously coarse and direct about her pleasures ... a born teacher'. Greer argued that it was not reform we needed but a revolutionary change in our social structure. 'To be in love is to be in dead trouble and to be deficient in the power of living and understanding the other person,' she said. 'The warning signal is when you're more anxious about losing the other person that seeing that they're happy'.

It was obvious even to the most dedicated Vogue editor that women who were world icons, such as Mrs Ghandi, Golda Meir or the Queen, were not going to disperse

Martha Graham
Cecil Beaton, 1976

left:
Kathleen Ferrier
Norman Parkinson, 1952

Maria Callas and Elsa Maxwell
1957

their wisdom through the glossy pages of Vogue. On the other hand, there were one or two fashion figures whose messages were inspiring to a world outside the couture.

The democratic president of modern fashion was Coco Chanel, who said 'Fashion does not exist unless it goes down into the streets. The fashion that remains in the salon has no more significance than a costume ball.' She has emerged as the most important and influential fashion designer of the century. A peasant girl from the Auvergne, orphaned at the age of six, she picked up on the changes forced on women with the First World War when women learned to run for a bus, wear trousers, shorten their skirts and smoke cigarettes. Those women had no idea they were inventing fashion, but Chanel saw that nothing would ever be the same again.

Her list of innovations is daunting. She put women into men's sweaters and shirts, and reinvented jersey – a fabric used for underclothes – as the chic daytime fabric. She put pockets in women's skirts and trousers, and weighted hems with tiny chains so that they wouldn't blow up. She talked about 'chic on the edge of poverty', hid fur inside coats and invented quilted silk and cire satin to replace mink and leather. She made fake jewellery more desirable than the real thing. She said that clothes must be packable and not need daily ironing. She borrowed the jackets of riding habits from her first known lover, 'Boy' Capel, and striped waistcoats from the footman's livery of her second, the Duke of Westminster. When she stepped off his yacht at Cannes, dressed all in white and navy, she introduced the suntan as the chic accessory of the rich and leisured. The Duke was the richest man in England, a handsome aristocrat whose shoelaces and newspaper were ironed every morning by his valet. He asked her to marry him, but she turned him down for something better: a career.

She foresaw that fashion would become a global conglomerate, and never minded her designs being copied. Uniquely among couturiers, she made no efforts to prevent it. She told Vogue in 1954, at the time of her first comeback, 'I am no longer interested in dressing a few hundred private clients: I shall dress thousands.' Far more influential than any later incarnation of the fashion house, she is still dressing millions.

Diana Cooper
Cecil Beaton, 1937

right:
Patricia Cunningham
Clifford Coffin, 1947

Bridget Riley
Peter Rand, 1966

left:
Germaine Greer
Snowdon, 1971

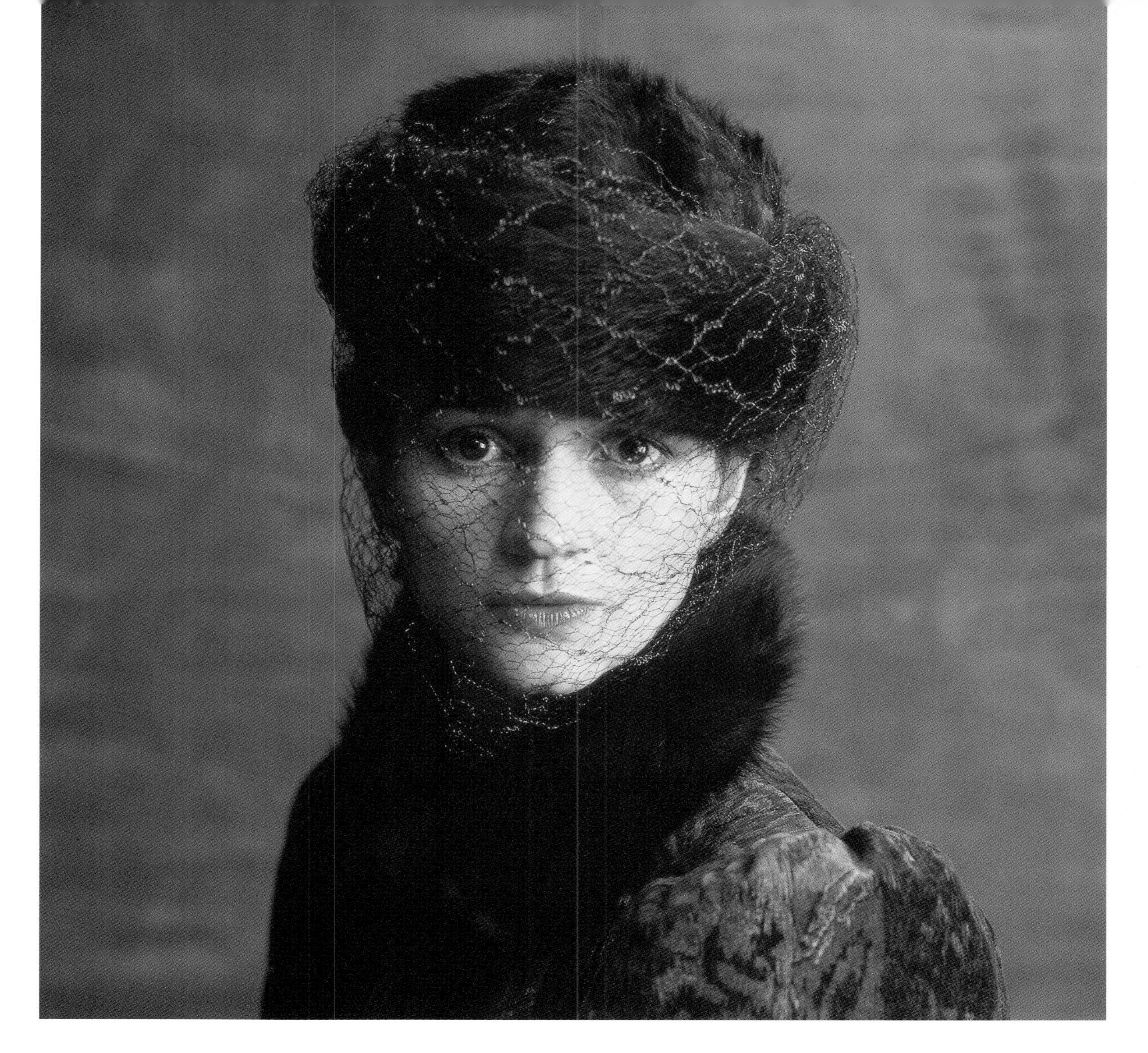

Marina Warner
Snowdon, 1982

left:
Antonia Fraser
Vernier, 1965

Margaret Thatcher
Snowdon, 1982

right:
Mother Teresa
John Downing, 1981

following pages, left:
Paloma Picasso
Oberto Gili, 1986
following pages, right:
Bianca Jagger
Eric Boman, 1974

4 muses

'More chic than Inès you cannot be,' said Karl Lagerfeld of his muse of the Eighties: and the split that followed between Karl and Inès de la Fressange did nothing to alter that fact. Lagerfeld laid the world of Chanel at her feet, but his queen of the runway finally left to get married, and to use her impeccable sense of style in her own highly successful design empire.

With her ragged black hair, sparkling black eyes and vivacity, the half Argentine, wholly aristocratic Inès de la Fressange was adopted by Lagerfeld as the irreverent image of Chanel for the decade. Her seven-year, one-million-franc contract to become the house muse was the best deal yet offered to a French model.

At a time when he was reinventing and parodying the Chanel legacy, Inès carried his vision through 'to the street' by modernizing the famous trademark jackets and chains, throwing them together with her own haphazard additions from antique clothes shops and flea markets. With all the resources of the rue Cambon at her disposal, the day that I met her, she was wearing her red velvet Chanel jacket with orange wool tights, ballet slippers – and nothing else.

She was always more than a mannequin. 'I always used to feel there was a question mark over me,' she once told me. 'What was I? Not exactly a model. Certainly not a designer.' Her steamroller charm extended the boundaries of what a model can mean. To her amazing looks she added all that her intelligence, confidence and eccentric bohemian background had given her, and became the toast of the international fashion world. She was soon playing hostess for the homosexual couturier, enchanting his business associates and sweetening the rounds of his promotional duties.

Her runway performances became entertainments. She would walk down the runway with her mongrel, Jim, wearing a quilted coat that matched her miniskirt. Spotting an empty seat in the front row of one Chanel show, she stepped off the runway, sat down, stretched out her legs – the legs that Lagerfeld said had launched every look of the 80s – and complained to her surprised neighbor about the rigors of a model's life. She endeared herself to working women everywhere by putting in what the French call 'the hours of the cleaning lady' and telling the press that dinner parties in the week are a terrible imposition ... 'Like from another century! You are supposed to get back from work, respond to the messages on the answering machine, answer your personal letters, and be at your friends' house at nine with your make-up on, your hair done, and a big smile on your face!'

The well-publicized split with Lagerfeld arose over her determination, against his command, to accept the invitation to personify Marianne, the national emblem

Inès de la Fressange
Albert Watson, 1985

regularly updated with the face currently judged the most beautiful in France. She thought it an honor: he said it was 'common'. To his evident surprise, the fashion magnate found his favorite quite adamant. She stood firm, and the argument went public in 1989.

A top model or muse generally embarks on an afterlife with a prince or a billionaire, and her career is swiftly forgotten. Jacques Fath's Bettina teamed up with Aly Khan, Fiona Campbell Walter married Baron von Thyssen, and Hattie Carnegie's favorite model, Pauline, married Baron de Rothschild. Inès married an old friend, Luigi d'Urso, and started her own design label and opened a successful chain of boutiques which sold clothes and decorative objects.

A muse needs more profile and social assurance than a model. Inès was able to have a second career through the very strength of character that had distinguished her from the start. It had led her to educate herself, and then throw the education away to become a model, then to transform the profession. It was only to be expected that the important but secondary role of muse would not detain her for long.

Karl Lagerfeld, now in his sixties, has long tried to find a muse to replace the irreplaceable Inès, and to update Chanel. There has been the baby doll blonde Claudia Schiffer, who never ventured beyond the role of supermodel, followed by the nose-beringed sculptor Stella Tennant. Currently, Amanda Harlech reigns supreme: a horsy Englishwoman who has decamped from leaking mansions in Shropshire and Wales to the Paris Ritz and Lagerfeld's ateliers.

Born Amanda Grieve, the barrister's daughter grew up in London and became the Zuleika Dobson of her era at Oxford before marrying Francis Ormsby-Gore in 1986. Shortly before the wedding, Lord Harlech, Francis' father, died in a car accident. Francis succeeded to the title, incurring crushing death duties of £1.6 million. The lure of fashion and city life and, perhaps, a comfortable wage, proved stronger than a life of penury in a stately home. 'Francis would often ask me why I didn't use some of my creative energy at home,' Amanda Harlech admitted to journalist Elizabeth Grice in 1999. The Harlechs stayed together long enough to have two children before divorcing in 1998.

Intense, highly strung and notoriously tricky, Amanda Harlech rims her blue eyes with kohl and lets her black hair run riot. As a freelancer for Vogue and a fashion editor on Harpers and Queen, she proved herself an accomplished stylist before meeting the novice designer John Galliano. She admired a dress he had made, and ended up by working for him for a dozen years as his style director and aide-de-camp. The call from Karl Lagerfeld

Amanda Harlech
Karl Lagerfeld, 1997

came just as Galliano, by then the star of Givenchy, was about to sign with Christian Dior. For whatever reason, she decamped to Chanel, where she now dances to Lagerfeld's tune.

'Amanda has a modern sensibility and she doesn't know the meaning of vulgar,' said Karl in February 1997. 'I'm not a woman. I don't wear the clothes. She can tell me what it is like.'

A designer's entire empire rests on his ability to lead fashion, and the more fantastic and spectacular his clothes, the more out of touch he can be. The original function of a muse was to wear the clothes to advantage in the real world. For the purposes of couture, a muse must also be a society figure who brings the designer's name to the attention of potential customers. One of the first, the Duchesse de Gramont, fulfilled this role for Madeleine Vionnet, the great French dressmaker of the 20s who invented the bias cut satin dress. Formerly the Princess Maria Ruspoli of Italy, the Duchesse became a famous Paris hostess who was said to have entertained 90,000 people in her lifetime. 'She was a real model, tall and beautiful,' said Madame Vionnet. 'When I was making a dress I had only to ask her to come and try it on and I knew exactly where it was wrong.'

Every muse fulfils a different role, and provides a cocktail of elements the couturier lacks. 'Loulou' de la Falaise, muse and greatest woman friend of Yves Saint Laurent, is alluring, international, articulate and the absolute opposite of the reclusive, somewhat fragile personality of the world-famous couturier.

Pierre Bergé, the mastermind behind the business side of Saint Laurent, has compared her to the famously elegant Mitza Bricard, who fulfilled a similar role for Christian Dior in the late 1940s and early 50s, saying that Loulou's function is also one of balance, and of 'grounding' the soaring visions of a virtuoso designer. Dior himself said that Madame Bricard was one of those people, increasingly rare, 'who make elegance their sole raison d'être' and that Bricard's exuberance perfectly balanced his own diffidence.

With Loulou's low, rusty voice, red hair and insolent green eyes, she is more fascinating than pretty; provocative, and as thin as a reed. Much more than an ideal figurehead, she sparks off the creative talents not only of Saint Laurent, but of a generation of fashion designers who unanimously regard her with awe. Like the exotic and tragically short-lived Tina Chow, the former wife of restaurateur Michael Chow, she inspired a whole raft of 70s fashionistas. Top shoe designer Manolo Blahnik gives one example. Spotting Loulou on the King's Road in London, in the summer of 1972, wearing a turban, poppies and thick cork-soled espadrilles, he went straight to his studio to design a collection of raffia platform shoes.

Loulou de la Falaise
Oberto Gili, 1986

From generations of the Falaise fashion dynasty, Louise, or Loulou as she became known, was intended for a debutante, but her grandmother neglected to put the usual mention in The Times, or add her name to the official list. Left out of the dances that would have bored her, in any case, Loulou kicked her heels in St John's Wood, London, until she met her first husband, Desmond FitzGerald, possessor of a unique inherited Irish title, the Knight of Glin. As 'the Madame FitzGerald', she decamped to his battlemented white castle on the banks of the Shannon. Recognizing at the outset his wife's low boredom threshold, FitzGerald organized house parties and imported planeloads of London friends for her entertainment. 'I've never seen anyone so captivated by fashion,' he said once. 'She was so excited by dressing up. Any excuse and out would come peacock feathers, strange belts, stage jewellery. Not that she spent a lot of money on clothes. It was all theatrical fantasy. She invented her own.'

The marriage fizzled out with an admirable lack of rancor, and in New York Loulou joined forces with Warhol and Halston and became a creature of the night. She met Saint Laurent in 1968, at a tea party at which they dressed up and Yves performed one of his famous fashion impersonations: probably his party piece, Coco Chanel. When Loulou returned to New York he sent her a crate of clothes from his 1940s-inspired ready-to-wear collection. Wonderful gifts kept arriving in the famous black and white boxes. Every time she went to Paris, she would drop in. Then, one day, Yves telephoned her and asked her to stay in Paris and work for him.

She still dresses from the cutting-room floor, and has been called by fashion designer Fernando Sanchez 'an artist of the safety pin. Three pins and two pieces of cloth, and she has four ravishing evening dresses.'

At the famous 70s weekend parties of Eric de Rothschild at the Chateau Lafitte, where fancy dress was compulsory, she would arrive with the pickings of the YSL atelier floor: feathers, gold lace, petticoats, hats, and artificial flowers. She styled the guests as Berlin cabaret stars or robots, billiard cues or circus performers ... and once appeared herself as a walking tree with branch limbs. Number 5, Avenue Marceau, is for her not the intimidating edifice of the most famous couture house in Paris, but a resplendent dressing-up box, the superlative version of the trunks of unworn clothes that her grandmother left behind after her death, to be distributed through the family.

'Life has its stages and epochs,' she once told me. 'I seem to have hit places at the right moment, when they needed new blood. There was London in the 60s, New York in the 70s, and Paris in the 80s.'

Catherine Deneuve
David Bailey, 1967

In France she finally put the pieces of her life together, reinventing herself and her outré brand of style. In due course she married again, to the son of the painter Balthus, becoming Loulou de La Falaise Klossowski.

If Loulou provided the style stimulus for Saint Laurent, the personification of.the ideal Saint Laurent customer was the beautiful and sophisticated Catherine Deneuve, who had and still has her own career as the most famous of French movie stars. She was well described by the Sunday Times Magazine journalist Francis Wyndham in 1968, when she was just breaking through to international recognition: 'She has a quick, rather literal mind, a brisk, graceful manner, and a firm, efficient character with a tendency towards melancholy ... Hard, yet capable of melting, she resembles that paradoxical dish, the chaud-froid. She is very French.'

She met the Vogue photographer David Bailey, in 1965, when he flew to Paris to photograph her in the nude for Playboy. She already had children by Roger Vadim and Marcello Mastroianni, both of whom she had neglected to marry. Racy, casual, witty, she is a respected member of the cabal of Parisian film-makers and intellectuals. She has a humor and vivacity which her enigmatic transparent film presence never suggested.

Bailey was in Paris again to photograph the collections when an old friend bet him ten bob he wouldn't propose to Deneuve. The wedding took place a few weeks later, Deneuve wearing a throwaway little black dress, with Mick Jagger as best man. Back in Bailey's house in Primrose Hill, London, Deneuve briefly played the role of housewife before returning to Paris. Not long afterwards, she telephoned him to tell him they were divorced. 'She said, "Now we can be lovers!",' he told me later. The marriage had begun and ended with a joke. Meanwhile, the famous film star had taken up her busy and interesting Parisian life again, continuing to star equally in French movies and in Yves' wonderfully elegant and flattering clothes.

A muse is always identified with the designer she inspires, but at the same time she is his opposite, supplying the elements that he lacks. Often she provides, too, an entrée to a world from which the designer may be excluded for reasons of age, sex or culture. Unique as these women are, everything depends on the perception of them from both the designer's and the public's point of view as bridging the gap between the drawing board and the woman who buys the clothes.

5 dynasties

Just as Shakespeare wrote, 'Rough winds do shake the darling buds of May': no beauty lasts for long and acknowledged beauties must become ex-beauties, unless for a few effort-filled years they can keep up with fashion. While today's media can make models famous overnight at ages when their mothers were still doing their homework, a star's spell in the spotlight can be over by the time she is 20. The fascinating exception is beauty that is passed on like a legacy from mother to daughter and beyond, establishing families of famous good looks that can last half a century or more.

Even to people who are not particularly subject to fashion or sex appeal, beauty acts like a magnet. The eye loves to dwell on haunting features, and a great photograph prompts the idle wish to identify the subject and find out more about her. Who is the slender blonde in blue satin at the head of the stairs? Is this her first ball? Is this the night that she will meet her lover? When the caption tells you only the name of the designer and the price of the dress, when the face is anonymous and the history unknown, there is a vacuum which the mind rushes to fill with fantasy. But memory is short. When you see the same model in a clothing catalog the next week, windblown on a beach, you will probably fail to recognize her.

But when you know that her name is Uma Thurman, that she is a movie star, and that your mother admired her mother, Nena Von Schlebrugge, 40 years ago, because she was one of the favorite models of Norman Parkinson, then the mysterious blonde enters the real world. She becomes a woman with a past, and therefore a future. You are sensitized to her, and pleased to be able to pick out her picture from a page of photographs taken at a movie premiere. It's fun to find out who she is living with, and what kind of a life she leads. Soon you will be buying a magazine because she is on the cover. Going through a cupboard one day, you find an old Vogue magazine with her mother Nena on the cover, and pause to examine the pure, surprised-looking face and pale pageboy hair, comparing her to her daughter.

Why it should be gratifying to trace the resemblance between a mother and daughter is a mystery, but even when a child is so young that her features are unformed, friends like to hang over the pram and remark 'She's so like her mother!' For anyone who is interested in fashion, there is a further fascination. Confronted with the photographs of two roughly similar women, both aged 20, what is it that betrays one face as belonging to the 1950s, and another as belonging to the 1900s? If the faces are approximately the same, what has transformed the look and made it of today?

The answer is compounded of all the elements that can be grouped under the heading of style: haircut, make-up or the lack of it, posture, the way the woman ignores or

previous pages:
Uma Thurman
Albert Watson, 1994

confronts the camera lens, her attitude. Her clothing opens up another file of options, chief of which is the question whether she is dressed for public or private observation. It wasn't so much that the models of Nena's generation, in the 1950s, were dressed like 'ladies': they were dressed to be seen in public. The stars of the millennium are dressed or partially undressed the way only their intimates would have seen them in any other era – whether with dirty hair and a petticoat dress, or in an old shirt and combat pants on a press trip to the Amazonian jungle. These enormous differences between pictures of the generations betray the context of our lives and times, never more so than when the similarities are strongly marked.

The last half century has given beauty a bad press. No wonder that, where beauty is a family precedent, the new generation is as likely to react against it as to rise to the challenge. Once, to be an acknowledged beauty in English society, you only had to be a pleasant-looking debutante, with a father rich enough to pay for a memorable coming out ball. These days, it takes a competitive nature and a sharp appreciation of how good looks can be turned to personal and commercial advantage. None of these prerequisites is supposed to cultivate happy families, and may positively discourage them. The high incidence of divorce, after all, has definitely deterred young lovers in the millennium from tying the knot. Examples such as Monroe and Diana suggest that far from guaranteeing love and happiness, beauty, attention and fame may lead directly to depression and rehab.

Since the explosion of the media in the 1970s and 80s, there have never been enough stars to go round. The press, who are always avid for new faces, especially when they can be coupled with famous names, do not wait to see if the offspring of the famous enter the public arena of their own accord. They pursue them even before they have finished their schooldays. But beauty is never down to the genes alone. Whatever a woman's natural and inherited advantages, her wares have to be advertised. 'Beauties' must be seen around and about, photographed and discussed. They must meet the press halfway. They must be seen to have a lively social life, and a presentable escort, preferably the offspring of an equally famous parent. When a rival candidate steals the limelight from them, and the papers lose interest, they must find a way of wrestling back public attention. When they read unwelcome comments about themselves, they must laugh through the tears and work up a snappy retort. From the very first mention of their name in The Times or Tatler, usually in a fleeting but friendly aside – 'Among the spectators at the Badminton Horse Trials was Lady Gabriella Windsor, the 18-year-old daughter of Prince and Princess Michael of Kent, who had borrowed an admirer's hat and looked a lot better than him in it' – daughters have to decide at once

Nena
Norman Parkinson, 1958

Enid Boulting
Norman Parkinson, 1950

right:
Ingrid Boulting
Norman Parkinson, 1970

previous pages, left:
Grace Kelly
Philippe Halsman, 1953
previous pages, right:
Caroline of Monaco
Patrick Lichfield, 1989

Jackie Kennedy
Harry Benson, 1961

right:
Lee Radziwill
Henry Clarke, 1960

previous pages, left:
Maxime de la Falaise
Clifford Coffin, 1949
previous pages, right:
The Falaise Family
Andre Rau, 1993

whether to rise to the occasion or whether to make a deliberate movement in the opposite direction.

That was the decision forced on Carolyn Bessette Kennedy when she married John Kennedy. Professionally employed for a time at the New York fashion house of Calvin Klein, Carolyn was an elegantly slim albino blonde. She agonized about her image, withdrew to private life and became something of a recluse. Nevertheless, she was well on her reluctant way to becoming an icon herself when the private plane piloted by her husband crashed on the way to a Kennedy wedding, killing both Kennedys and her sister. Their loss stunned the world.

For sheer longevity as aristocrats of style, the de la Falaise family are the most famous of fashion dynasties. Born to glamour since the 1930s, four generations of women have risen to the occasion. The line originated with the Marquis de La Falaise de Coudray, who married Gloria Swanson, star of the 1920s, and then Constance Bennett, movie star of the 1940s. It was his younger brother, Alain, who married Maxime Birley, and brought her from New York to complete her fashion and style education in Paris just after the war, at the time of the New Look.

Maxime was a young crop-headed comtesse, tall and thin enough to carry off the most extreme clothes of an extreme period. Her contemporaries still remember her appearance at a ball in a dress with a screen of black ostrich feathers that completely hid her face, and at a dinner with Aly Khan in a sheath bustle dress so tight that she couldn't sit down at the table. No wonder that her daughter, Loulou de La Falaise Klossowski, was to become the outrageously chic muse of Yves Saint Laurent some 30 years later. With her rusty bobbed hair, scornful green eyes and feline face, Loulou has, since her first meeting with Saint Laurent in 1968, inhabited the world of inspiration between the couturier's dreams and the first snip of the scissors.

Then there is Lucie, the pretty blue-eyed daughter of the furniture designer Alexis de La Falaise. Small, with fine features and a cameo profile, she turned 19 just as Saint Laurent was ransacking Paris for a new face for the image of his cosmetics and perfume empire. Even the teenage Anna Baladine Rose Cassimira Klossowski, Loulou's daughter, is growing into an acknowledged beauty.

6 *models*

'Apart from athletics', said Cindy Crawford once, 'modelling is the only profession where after the first two or three years you can only get worse.'

For half of its history, modelling has been unglamorous and badly paid. The early models that we remember were pioneers, snatching glamour from decidedly inelegant situations. Even the supermodels have suffered. Karl Lagerfeld put a rude end to Claudia Schiffer's career with a press announcement brimming over with his usual diplomacy and finesse. 'She is part of another world, another time ... she no longer has the right look. She should have been a star of the silent screen.'

Early models, employed by the couturiers to try on samples for the benefit of customers, were no better than living dummies. They wore substantial boned corsets and black silk body-concealers, and had the same status as the newest seamstress in the atelier. These anonymous young women, not specially pretty but with good figures, were paid a pittance. Whenever anything was needed, they slipped off their wraps, put on their threadbare coats and ran errands.

In the 1910s, Lucile was the first fashion house to realize the potential of models. With establishments in Paris, London, New York and Chicago, Lucile was owned and run by Lady Duff Gordon, the sister of Elinor Glyn. Duff Gordon designed dresses as sensational and extravagant as any of the designs from the Russian Ballet, and costumed the Ziegfeld Follies. Her evening dresses turned women into glittering dragonflies, with beaded trains and fountains of ostrich feathers. A businesswoman through and through, she came to realize that clients were more likely to part with their money if they saw her dresses looking their best on a beauty with society manners, rather than a half-starved gamine. The statuesque Dolores, who married a millionaire, was the first model to be known to clients by her name. Other Lucile models, Hebe and the exotic Sumurun, went on to model for Captain Molyneux, who was trained by Duff Gordon and came to dress Marina, the Duchess of Kent.

Fashion marketing advanced a stage when Jean Patou travelled to New York to find wholesome American blondes who would appeal to the transatlantic buyers. Brigid Keenan discovered the advertisements that Patou placed in the New York papers. He was looking for girls who were 'smart, slender, with well-shaped feet and ankles and refined of manner'. He returned to Paris with a handful of immaculate young Americans in pleated skirts and pink silk stockings; one was Edwina Prue, who became the Baroness d'Erlanger.

The gentle, courteous Christian Dior cherished his mannequins, who worshipped him in return. 'They alone give life to my dresses,' he said. 'I cannot think of one

Wenda
Norman Parkinson, 1951

without the other.' They were, he considered, a vital part of his success, when his New Look of 1947 brought him one and a half times more orders than were taken by all the rest of the Paris haute couture. Of his favorite mannequins, known by their Christian names only, he said that the model France was the greatest of all because she was typically Parisienne, but the pet of the House was Lucky. 'She thinks and translates the intentions of the dress,' said Dior. 'She does not wear it, she acts it.' With her eyelids drawn out with a flick of black and her vivid brunette looks, he used her to carry off his most lighthearted and extreme fashions and designs, such as the 'Easter egg' hairdo from one spring collection. She had set her heart on being a model, and, considering herself not pretty enough, had undergone a whole series of cosmetic operations before presenting herself to him. She died in 1963.

Each couturier had his own favorite model, but Jacques Fath's ideal, the red-haired Bettina, became a national favorite. Always the first choice of the great French photographer Henri Cartier-Bresson, she had a parallel career as a cover girl. The pathos of her story, like a novel by Colette, made her an object of affection throughout France. She was on duty at Fath one day, when Prince Aly Khan, brother of the Aga Khan, arrived with his fiancée, Rita Hayworth, to choose her a trousseau. Equally red-headed but more elegant than Hayworth, the mannequin certainly caught the eye of Aly Khan as she modelled all the clothes that the movie star would be wearing on her honeymoon. In due course, when Hayworth had flounced back to Hollywood complaining of boredom, Bettina ended up as Aly Khan's long-term mistress. She adored him. For years, hoping he would ask her to marry him, she waited patiently and forgivingly on the sidelines of his philandering life, knowing herself to be second best, until he was tragically killed in a car crash in 1960.

It was not just the designers who discovered and promoted these beauties, giving the modelling profession its glamour and prestige and providing the means by which these often quite ordinary girls were able to marry rank and wealth. Each Vogue photographer had his favorite model who lit up the lens and helped produce great pictures. As John French, the most famous of the British fashion photographers of the 50s, was to say 'There are girls with whom you can take hundreds of shots, but the session becomes dead. Then there are girls whose alchemy is right. Their personality suddenly bubbles, they react and make that fantastic rapport happen'.

The great Vogue photographer of the late 30s, Horst P. Horst, made Lyla Zelensky into a teenage star. Interviewed by journalist Colin McDowell, she remembered how she was dressed and made up to look at least 35: 'It was still quite rare for Vogue and Harper's

Bazaar to use professional models. They preferred the clothes to be photographed on society women and their daughters, because they felt that they moved in the correct world and would wear the clothes better. There were no model schools or anything like that. You just had to know how to wear clothes. The image was very sophisticated, and you had to be aware of how to move and compose yourself in front of the camera.'

Vogue's wish to show clothes on society women was at loggerheads with the determination of the photographers to use their own trusted favorites. The photographers were getting more powerful. Postwar Paris saw the rise of a generation of brilliant American photographers who usually preferred to work with American models. There was Irving Penn and Lisa Fonssagrives, whom he later married; Henry Clarke and Suzy Parker, who became Chanel's favorite model in the late 50s; Richard Avedon – who said 'I am always a little in love with my girls' – and Dovima. Parodied in the Audrey Hepburn/Fred Astaire movie Think Pink – with Richard Avedon as high-powered visual consultant – some of these relationships moved beyond the studio, just as they were to do in the 60s when David Bailey chose the career of a fashion photographer solely to get close to the most beautiful girls in the world.

Marshalling the cosmetic techniques of Hollywood and matching the technological advances of photography and printing with a higher quality of glossy paper, Vogue began to select its models with the care of a director who auditions hundreds for a prize movie role. These women became very familiar to Vogue readers. We might not have known the name of the girl standing haughtily in front of a country house, holding the leads of a couple of greyhounds groomed as finely as she was herself, but we watched out for her and recognized her a month later, in a satin ballgown by a moonlit fountain – the photographer, perhaps, Norman Parkinson, the model his wife Wenda. In a way, their namelessness and lack of context only added to their mystery and made them more accessible to our own aspirations.

Now that designers and fashion editors had recognized the crucial role of models, the job acquired more cachet than being an actress. In 1955, in the whole of London, there were no more than a few hundred reasonably successful models. But by 1961, there were over 6000, and English girls were at the top. The Americans, particularly, admired their meticulous grooming off duty, their untemperamental approach to work and their impeccable English accents. Modelling suddenly become the prestige profession for women, and a shortcut to a fantasy marriage. Fiona Campbell Walter, with her county hauteur, was 'as finely bred as a champion greyhound', according to Cecil Beaton, and looked as if she was too grand to need a salary – as she soon was when she became Baroness von Thyssen, the wife of one of

Fiona Campbell Walter
Henry Clarke, 1951

Simone d'Aillencourt
Henry Clarke, 1957

left:
Jeannie Patchett
Norman Parkinson, 1950

the richest men in the world. Sally Croker-Poole married the Aga Khan. Bronwen Pugh, Balmain's favorite house model, married Viscount Astor and became chatelaine of Cliveden, one of the stateliest of English country houses. None of these marriages, however, was to last. Long after Cliveden's involvement in the Profumo Affair, from which her late husband never recovered, Bronwen Pugh lives today, a virtual recluse, in a Pentecostal retreat.

In the first years of the 60s, Vogue's older editors became alarmed to find the pages increasingly full of sexy young models just out of the schoolroom. They thought readers would be alienated. And so they created Mrs Exeter, a fictional character designed to prevent the older readers from feeling neglected. But while Mrs Exeter was attending a grand-daughter's christening in navy shantung with touches of white, or going on a spring cruise in a greige silk duster coat, David Bailey was turning Vogue into his personal vehicle for sex and fame and money. The momentous first meeting with Jean Shrimpton took place in the studio where Brian Duffy was photographing Shrimpton for a Kellogg's cornflakes advertisement. 'He was taking the picture against a blue background,' remembered Bailey. 'It was like her blue eyes were just holes drilled through her head to the paper behind. I thought she was the most amazing thing I had ever seen. And Duffy looked at me straightaway and said, "Forget it! You don't stand a chance. She's too posh for you." And I thought "We'll see about that."'

Bailey and Shrimpton turned fashion pictures into portraits full of sexual imagery. Stately houses were replaced by street markets and studio floors where Shrimpton sprawled, skirts thigh-high, sometimes toying with a gun or cuddling a teddy bear. The pictures, ripped out of Vogue, ended up in the oddest places: pinned on garage walls, in canteens and prison cells.

At about this time, Cherry Marshall, owner of the English modelling agency that handled Bronwen Pugh, Paulene Stone and Patti Boyd, was demanding $60 a day when her models worked in New York, or 5 guineas an hour back at home. But even this was considered too much by the glossy magazines, who held a cabal before issuing a joint ultimatum. No model who wanted to appear on Vogue pages would be paid more than 2 guineas an hour, or 10 guineas a day. The models were trapped. No-one would turn down the prestige jobs, and so they resigned themselves to making up the money doing advertising.

Anne St Marie
Henry Clarke, 1955

right:
Adele Collins
Norman Parkinson, 1959

right:
Barbara Goalen
Anthony Dennery, 1951

below:
Lucky
1963

But, just as the stinginess of the Hollywood studios would fall before the power of movie stars in the 70s, the Supermodels would get their own back in the 80s.

Although it would seem that the first supermodels were Jean Shrimpton and Twiggy, the child model with a naturally sophisticated face, neither had any power over their own careers. Shrimpton has admitted that she hated every minute of her fame, and it was years before Twiggy emerged from the aegis of her protector and shrewd manager Justin de Villeneuve. Jerry Hall and Marie Helvin were the first models with clout, but they were roller-coastered to the top by the men they partnered. Helvin married Bailey, and Hall acquired rock 'n' roll glory by marrying Mick Jagger.

When Linda Evangelista said 'I don't get out of bed for less than $10,000', the real supermodel was born. The first of her breed, it was Evangelista with her vivid, delicate face – she could be a fiery Bohemian princess or a young Sophia Loren from the back streets of Naples – who broke through the model contracts ceiling to raise her catwalk fee to an incredible $20,000, provoking the president of French fashion's governing body the Chambre Syndicale, Pierre Bergé, to thunder to the press about 'the crazy prices that models are asking now'. For commercials, her basic shooting fee was $10,000 a day. American Vogue's booking agent of the day, Preston Westenburg, explained: 'These kinds of fees are possible now because of worldwide buy-outs, time limitations, usages, billboards ... it's endless. But only five or six girls in the world can earn sums like that.' Vogue embargos on the top models prevented them from working for rival magazines, and contract fees went through the roof.

Evangelista, a Catholic from Toronto, pioneered the tough line, a policy aided by her short-term marriage to the then boss of her agency, Gerald Marie of Elite. The days when magazines used to book five or six girls for a shoot, choose one and keep the rest sitting were gone for good. Supermodel attitude was born. Evangelista wouldn't be photographed with any other model. Cindy Crawford wouldn't wear high necks. Naomi Campbell would turn up hours late. And if a photographer was getting it wrong, a supermodel would tell him how to take the picture, or walk out.

In the 90s, all fashion selling became indirect. The designer sold lifestyle, the couture frock on the catwalk sold the ready-to-wear, the glossy catalogue sold status, and the model sold it all. She made videos with rock stars and movies with actors, she signed £2 million perfume contracts, she charged fees for her appearance at parties, she was an MTV heroine.

The supermodel is evidently going to be with us for some time to come.

Jean Shrimpton
Cecil Beaton, 1964

right:
Anne Gunning
Norman Parkinson, 1956

Lana Ogilvy
Snowdon, 1989

right:
Peggy Moffitt
William Claxton, 1966

following pages, left:
Jerry Hall
Norman Parkinson, 1975
following pages, right:
Iman
John Swannell

ВОГ
СССР
1975

IMAN

Linda Evangelista
Patrick Demarchelier, 1987

right:
Cindy Crawford
Arthur Elgort, 1995

Naomi Campbell
Arthur Elgort, 1995

7 stars

Glamour is one of those properties that few attain, and nobody keeps. As it slipped from profession to profession over the momentous, changeable 20th century, the spotlight fell on a strange variety of stars.

At the beginning, glamour itself was a doubtful commodity in the aspirational world of Vogue. It belonged chiefly to actresses and entertainers, and most of all it was beyond the pale because it was the province of the oldest profession. The grandes cocottes of Paris were notorious women who dressed and lived in flamboyant, outrageous style just as long as they were young and beautiful enough to attract rich and titled men. They themselves were enslaved and exploited and, in their turn, they enslaved and exploited other people. They were outside society, the great uninvited, and at the same time had to maintain the highest profile to get themselves noticed. Society women loathed them, not only because of the marital suspicions they raised, but also because of the cocottes' public scraps with lovers and rivals, their fabulous jewels and the numbers of suicides they inspired by taunting and frustrating younger, often penniless sons. The wonderful pictures of these beautiful and spectacularly dressed women, taken by Henri Lartigue at fashionable parade grounds such as Longchamps and the Bois de Boulogne, were the inspiration for Cecil Beaton's designs for Audrey Hepburn in My Fair Lady (see page 7).

The First World War brought jobs for women, and the spotlight fell instead on society girls in dashing uniforms. Vogue could use these new stars for portraits, but not yet as mannequins for the new Paris frocks. These continued to be seen on musical comedy actresses, ballerinas and theatrical divas, who were delighted to show off the fanciful dresses designed for their new shows, or on loan from the couturiers Patou, Callot or Lucile. Punctuating page after page of fashion drawings, these early photographs provided the magazine's most memorable fashion input, while society beauties in their own clothes had their far duller, far less fashionable portraits taken by Hoppe, Hugh Cecil and Bertram Park.

The gap was bridged by Gaby Deslys, the glamour queen of the Paris stage famous for her towering feather head-dresses, who was photographed in the crowd at Ascot. Since her declaration that 'Money is a woman's only bulwark against the world' she was loved and followed by the press, who liked to list her fantastic collection of jewellery. Among these was a rope of pearls as long as herself from King Manuel of Portugal. She died with a last great theatrical gesture, leaving her money 'to the poor of Marseilles'.

Paris was the centre of the world of arts, and took the lead in all categories except for films. It was said that the time lag between avant-garde France and educated

right:
Merle Oberon
1933

below:
Sarah Bernhardt

England was about 12 years, and between educated England and the masses another two at least. Would-be stars came to France from all over the world to have international status conferred or denied. Once they had made it in Paris, these originals knew that they could make it anywhere. The international stars most frequently seen in Vogue at the end of the First World War were Irene Castle and her husband Vernon, brilliant dancing partners from New York, who had made famous such dances as the tango, the one-step and the Castle walk.

As far as Vogue's British readers of the day were concerned, the new American movie stars were outrageous extroverts, never to be taken seriously. The woman who had given them this clear impression was the biggest star of the 20s, Gloria Swanson. She was already a symbol of movie bad taste when she secured her social position by marrying a titled Frenchman, the Marquis de la Falaise de Coudray, 'a docile nobleman with a reckless taste in spats'. Returning to her palatial house in Hollywood, she installed a bevy of footmen and dressed them in a livery that might have come from one of her own movies about the court of Louis XIV. Visiting producers and directors were astonished to be received by a line-up of lackeys in powdered wigs and satin breeches.

While Hollywood was in its infancy, the London stage was long established with a rich cocktail of popular musical shows, classic plays and the new light comedies. In the mid 20s you could see Sybil Thorndike in Bernard Shaw's Nobel Prize-winning play Saint Joan, or a Cochran review. You could choose from a variety of comedies, the best being the star vehicles for Tallulah Bankhead – whose female fans regularly choked the West End – or the great draws of their day, the Noël Coward musicals, full of good lyrics and catchy tunes, with perfect timing and glamorous stars.

The fashion and sociology writer, the late James Laver, called the camera 'the first engine for imposing types of beauty' and pointed out, in a Vogue feature, that one curious result of the power of the movies had been the spread of type consciousness. Women wondered for the first time if they were the Clara Bow or the Dietrich type, and in Vogue, many of the models were recognizable copies of the stars, displaying Garbo's plucked eyebrows, Joan Crawford's crimson bow tie of a mouth, or the platinum hair of Jean Harlow. The unattainable glamour of stars like Vivien Leigh in Selznick's three-hour Gone with the Wind was the wistful side of the threadbare 30s, in reaction to the decline of world trade and the collapse of markets, and escapism the name of the game that Vogue was playing.

Only 20 years after the war to end all wars, peace was extinguished again. The First World War had changed the role of women, giving them jobs and independence,

Marlene Dietrich
Steichen, 1935

left:
Anna Pavlova

cigarettes and trousers. After 1918, society had never gone back to the rigid double standards of Edwardian days, and the Roaring Twenties had completed the metamorphosis of women, bringing them contraception, liberation and fun. The Second World War brought a new ideal, and different stars. These were rather more like the women in their audiences – fairly natural looking, and determinedly upbeat. In Britain, the Queen decided to dress like her subjects, conforming with the official line on austerity dressing and fabric restrictions, and following her lead, society stars packed away their cocktail dresses and went back to the land.

Vogue readers dressed down and saved their cosmetics for a rare evening out when their boyfriends or husbands returned on leave. As American movie stars of the robust Betty Grable and Constance Bennett type eclipsed the exotic Garbos and Pola Negris of former years, Vogue became aware that something unique was happening. Stars were copying ordinary people, rather than the other way around. Cinemagoers put their exotic fantasies on hold, identifying instead with tranquil, classic beauties who you could have seen in the high streets of any provincial market town, changing a library book or pausing for a cup of tea: the gentle but heroic Anne Todd, Deborah Kerr, or Celia Johnson.

The new morality didn't last long. The moment the war was over, fantasy and glamour came flooding back. Just as women now longed for Christian Dior's New Look of 1947, with its rustling petticoats, handspan waists and sweeping skirts, they yearned for sentimental, romantic stories and stars who would guarantee to provide vicarious excitement. Their wish was granted by the movies.

Before the war, we knew little about the stars except the names of their latest husbands. Occasionally there was the hint of a scandal in which drugs and alcohol were never named, but usually implicit. The next thing movie fans learnt from their movie magazines was that these stars had been dropped by their studios. They were seldom if ever heard of again. Now the paparazzi, using telephoto lens, dogged the new Italian stars and soon spread their intrusive presence to Paris and Los Angeles. Stars had to watch their step, but they were no longer without a measure of power of their own.

As movies reached bigger and bigger audiences, stars began to wield that power. By the 1950s, a proportion were on friendly terms with the Mafia who operated the

Pola Negri
Steichen, 1925

right:
Margot Fonteyn
Cecil Beaton, 1954

American leisure industry, and they hobnobbed with presidents and kings. The subtext to their starring roles added hugely to their appeal. When Frank Sinatra played a hack journalist or a gambler or a backstreet detective, it was fun to know he dined at the White House. When Monroe sang 'Happy Birthday Mister President' to Jack Kennedy, we might not have known she was his mistress, and his brother's mistress, but we knew the song was loaded with innuendo.

Stars became the ornaments of upper-crust American culture and a few such as Warren Beatty, Jane Fonda and Robert Redford became heavily involved in the political life of the country. Clint Eastwood, while saying that he would never run for president because 'with my past, I wouldn't last two weeks', became a popular mayor of the county where he had his country house.

Each side conferred a quality that was of value to the other. It was an even-handed exchange of status and popularity. The actors climbed into society, the politicians won the popular vote. The stars had become the new aristocracy, adding social clout to wealth and public adulation. Like royalty itself, they could highlight whatever issues appealed to them: scientology, Buddhism, or the saving of the American landscape. In Britain, the Windsors continued to indulge a theatrical streak most pronounced in the Queen Mother and in Princess Margaret. Over the next few decades they were to invite to the palace an assortment of British comedians, producers and actors ranging from the Crazy Gang and the Goons to Andrew Lloyd Webber – in whose company the television production head Prince Edward earned his showbiz apprenticeship. Such entertainers as Peter Sellers, Harry Secombe and Simon Ward counted themselves as close acquaintances.

Britain had emerged from the turbulent last years of the 1950s a new country. 'In that period' wrote the American journalist John Crosby in the Daily Telegraph color supplement, 'youth captured this ancient island and took command in a country where youth had always before been kept properly in its place. Suddenly the young own the town.' Pop singers, photographers, actors, pop artists, hairdressers, restaurant owners, writers and designers all seemed to be in their mid twenties, and the new European movie stars had a leggy, adolescent look. Epitome of the new Lolita phenomenon was Brigitte Bardot, the

Katharine Hepburn
Cecil Beaton

Vivien Leigh
Rawlings, 1937

sensuous star of And God Created Woman, a mixture of the sexy and babyish in pink gingham and ribbon-tied broderie anglaise, long blonde hair tumbling round her face with its heavy eyelashes and pale pink, pouting lips.

But no star ever had such an impact on couture as Audrey Hepburn. Seven years after her death at 64, stores around the world are still stocked from her wardrobe: little black dresses with boat necks, lampshade hats that cast a shadow from shoulder to shoulder, ballet slippers with black leggings, skinny black turtlenecks with heavy sunglasses, chopped cream sweaters, pale mackintoshes to wear with black tights and scarves crossed over under the chin and tied in the nape of the neck. Audrey Hepburn could make any jewellery look real, just as Elizabeth Taylor could make any diamond look fake. When the two stars met at a premiere, Hepburn pointed to Taylor's largest and latest diamond and naughtily asked "Kenneth Lane?" – naming one of the best known of fake jewellery designers. But Taylor was quick witted, too. "No!" she shot back. "Richard Burton."

Hepburn was the daughter of a formidable Dutch baroness and an austere English banker, and her childhood in Nazi-occupied Holland was bleak. From it came the ambition and contrivance that her modest manner never betrayed. Her lovely deep voice with its absurdly slow, childish rhythm was the product of many elocution lessons. Some said she had the corners of her mouth slit to give her lips a smiling tilt. From Hepburn into our beauty vocabulary went her 'rat-nibbled' fringe, beige rather than pink lipstick, sweeping false eyelashes, eyes drawn out with a heavy line of black greasepaint, black-pencilled eyebrows, a lipline drawn outside the actual contours to enhance the mouth.

She was spotted in the chorus line of a 1949 London musical, Sauce Tartare, by theatre critic Milton Shulman, who wrote "She was as conspicuous as a fresh carnation on a shabby suit". When 78 year old Colette saw her on the Monte Carlo beach, the only girl with a flat chest and a black one-piece bathing suit, the famous French author pointed a finger and said "That's my Gigi!" Colette had casting approval over the Broadway staging of her most celebrated novella, and launched Hepburn as a star.

She eventually found the love of her life, Robert Wolders, although she never married him, having two divorces behind her. She lived in a manoir by the side of Lake Lucerne, where she was to be found gardening in a big straw hat with an apron wound twice around her tiny waist. In her final years, she spent her energies on volunteer work for UNICEF. She had returned from a gruelling trip to Somalia when the Cedars Sinai Medical Center confirmed that she had cancer. Givenchy sent his jet to bring her home for her last Christmas.

Claire Bloom
Anthony Denney, 1953

Jeanne Moreau
Dave Budnick, 1962

right:
Lauren Bacall
Paul Himmel, 1954

192857 ROMA

Faye Dunaway
J. Schatzberg, 1968

right:
Shirley McLaine
David Bailey, 1965

Hepburn herself never regretted that her well-born looks and manners had limited her choice of roles. 'It's all been sex and violence in the movies these last few years,' she said towards the end of her life. 'I'm far too scrawny to strip and I hate guns, so I'm better off out of it.'

But, for Vogue readers at least, a whole new category of stars was opening up – and one with a future. The best guarantee that any magazine will sell out is to put a beautiful, but more importantly, a familiar face on the cover. Repetition of a face through screen or print finally convinces. We become used to it, then sensitized to it, then addicted. The more photographs we have seen of a certain face, and the more we fantasize or know about the person, the more photographs of her we want to see. During the lifetime of Princess Diana, it was common magazine knowledge that nothing sold the magazine so well as yet another picture of the world's already most photographed cover girl.

The public had come to recognize the features of queens and society women through the shadowy medium of early newsprint, when photographs were called 'smudges'. Later they had seen those women in motion through the cinema newsreels of social events such as Ascot and movie premieres. Now, sophisticated cosmetic techniques learned from Hollywood were matched with better paper and improvements in photography and printing. The Vogue editors and photographers accordingly began to select their fashion models to become the stars of the magazine.

These girls were not intended to be flash-in-the-pan faces, but the personification of Vogue fashion. They were the stars without a name. Ten more years, and the reader knew the names of the top models of the day, and even who their boyfriends were, all without having to be told. While the names would be written in large type across the fashion pages of newspapers, Vogue still refrained. Vogue had two reasons. Society girls and celebrities would agree to portraits by Bailey or Avedon, and would queue up to be dressed from the newest boutique and transformed by the most skilful make-up artists in the business, just as long as they weren't being used as anonymous models. And the accounts department was aware that if you turn models into stars, it won't be long before their agents turn around and demand movie star money. It wasn't, and they did.

It was the continuing emphasis on their faces in Vogue that made models into something more. Jean Shrimpton and Twiggy were mobbed in the streets, and the photographers themselves became stars as they focused on their favorites. As the urbane gentlemen of the 1950s – Parkinson, Penn, Avedon – were succeeded by the wit and

Barbra Streisand
Cecil Beaton, 1969

Brigitte Bardot
Sam Lévin

left:
Sophia Loren
David Bailey, 1965

Julie Christie
David Bailey, 1967

raunchiness of the 1960s – Bailey, Duffy, Donovan – they brought younger and more original beauties into the fashion pages of Vogue. In the magazine you could now see the daughters of farmers and greengrocers, pearly queens, diplomats, foreign and British aristocracy, and even African chieftains.

Supermodels and film stars were neck and neck in the popularity stakes by the mid 1980s. Actresses found that they had lost their hold on the glamour market, and that the hundreds of fans waiting on the pavements on either side of the red carpet were just as excited to see Naomi or Cindy as they used to be when they spotted the movie stars.

Actresses drew apart in dudgeon from run-of-the-mill fashion magazines, deliberately avoided couture and refused to model clothes. They wanted gravitas and more respect, and they soon knew where to go. Investigative journalism was in its heyday, journalism the chic career and Tina Brown's Vanity Fair the hot magazine of its day. The agents of the big movie stars sought weighty 8,000 and 10,000 word profiles on their behalf, and agreed to an extraordinary degree of exposure to get it. Journalists who interviewed these actors for Vanity Fair or Vogue were granted whole days in their company. They were allowed to fly in the stars' private planes, follow them to parties, grill their families and friends, inspect and criticize their houses and see the stars in jeans and bare feet. All too often this degree of exposure only managed to reveal that there was little to say. The public began to realize that no matter that she's paid millions of dollars a film, at the end of the day a movie star is all too often just an actor with a photogenic face.

The reaction against the star business that followed was played out on both sides. Writers of the Lynn Barber school used the exposure to mock and belittle. A writer who didn't find something to criticize was accused of selling out to cronyism. The actors couldn't refuse interviews altogether, committed as they were to publicity clauses in their contracts, but, stung by the ingratitude of journalists to whom they had opened their hearts, they began to look for protection in causes that were above reproach. Following the time-honored example of royalty, they tried to tie in interviews with copious acknowledgement of their work for charity. Noblesse oblige, and readers soon began to tire of photographs of the stars in shorts and camouflage T-shirt, embracing starving Ethiopian children or Indian orphans. Latest addition to world worthiness is the former Spice Girl, Geri Halliwell, now frequently photographed as a goodwill ambassador for the UN Population Fund.

Early movie stars from the silent screen were chosen for their beauty alone. For a decade or so longer, they only had to be able to speak and behave like a celebrity. The

Gladys Cooper
Anthony Buckley

Monica Vitti
David Bailey, 1965

Bond girls from the 60s harked back to these early days when pulchritude and a lovely face were enough. The role of 007's latest often went to a fashion model who was keen to begin a new and better-paid career in films. With only a few minutes of screen exposure in which to tumble about in bed with Roger Moore or Sean Connery before meeting a nasty screen death, she had only the briefest opportunity to prove she could act. The fact that remarkably few of these went on to make more films speaks for itself. The professionalism, intelligence and discipline required for today's movie-making means that it is more likely that a clever woman with an interesting face will land the role, than one who is beautiful but awkward on live camera. From many examples, there are three notable names: Meryl Streep, Glenn Close and Emma Thompson.

Films, as Andy Warhol might have said, are the new books. Acting now is of such a naturalistic standard and films are so close to life in plot and settings that glamour is of less importance than the ability to involve the audience in the plot. The stars we want to see give to the audience a sense of inhabiting for a couple of hours a bigger, faster, more powerful world. When the audience wants to identify with a star today they want to participate in the predicaments portrayed in brilliantly transparent acting. A star wins public adulation not only because she has a fascinating and familiar face, but because of where she takes us in her films. It is the character with which they emerge from their movies that counts more than glamour, and where the star has it all, the financial rewards are incredible: Julia Roberts received a cool 20 million dollars for her role in the absorbing, gritty Erin Brokovitch.

Stars are made by their fans, and the nature of fans has also changed. They don't sublimate their feelings about the stars as they used to do, by sending off for autographed portraits or collecting cuttings. Superb actors, lovely to look at, personalities of the calibre of Gwyneth Paltrow, Meg Ryan, Cameron Diaz, Julia Roberts, Kate Winslet and Michelle Pfeiffer are stars whose names are enough to 'sell' the movies they are in. We go to see them for their acting, because they guarantee that the film will be good. That is box office in 2000, and it is the definition of a movie star today.

Stars have lost their mystery, but they have won out over the glamorous supermodels by becoming more interesting, sophisticated and connected to our own lives.

right:
Charlotte Rampling
Clive Arrowsmith, 1970

following pages, left:
Nicole Kidman
T. Munro, 1998
following pages, right:
Gwyneth Paltrow
Mario Testino, 1998

8

exotics/eccentrics

Some of the most fashion-conscious women in the world have chosen to dress in a bizarre, rather than a decorative manner. Diana Vreeland, once editor-in-chief of Vogue, then curator of fashion at the Metropolitan Museum of Art, wore children's strap and button shoes, and had the insoles buffed daily with an elk horn. Italian Vogue fashion editor Anna Piaggi wears extraordinary clothes every day, and might give a dinner party dressed in a bib-front kitchen apron with zouave trousers and a soft bow tie, or walk about in Paris in a highwayman's costume with a frilled and embroidered evening cape. Isabella Blow, originally from Tatler and now fashion director of the Sunday Times' Style section, has been seen cooking in a 30s Schiaparelli monkey-fur coat.

There are two kinds of eccentric dressers. There are those who, having once discovered the way they feel comfortable, would dress the same way on a desert island. Then there are the women who cannot bear to pass unperceived. Like transvestites, the thrill they feel depends not just on the drag, but in the reactions they provoke. Ida Rubinstein, the Russian ballerina who came to Paris with Diaghilev and was left permanently exiled after the Russian Revolution, would walk straight down the middle of the road, stopping the traffic in the most fantastic hats and trains that the couturier Paul Poiret could devise for her. The Marquesa Casati, with her glittering black-ringed eyes and mop of orange hair, was followed about in her native Rome by a black page in a turban and 18th-century livery, with satin hose and buckled shoes. Lest she should go unnoticed, she sometimes led a leopard on a diamond-studded leash; a monkey and several snakes were permanent lodgers in her house. She won the admiration of the poet Gabriel d'Annunzio, for whom she left her husband in 1919, and continued to dress and behave so strangely that Augustus John once remarked to Cecil Beaton that she would end by being stuffed and put in a glass case.

Eccentrics such as these are one-offs, distinct from the head-turners of 80 years later. Unlike the punk, who sees himself as a member of a rebel urban tribe, in his green Mohican, chained legs and spike-studded leather bracelet, these women make no kind of political statement. Sometimes they turn their hands to art or design, but the real production is always the same: themselves. If someone dared to copy them, they would swiftly move on to even wilder sartorial shores. Mrs Reginald Fellowes, a woman whose clothes stood out even in the unconventional 30s, and was often seen in a sequin tuxedo with a green carnation, once found herself at a dinner party with another woman in the same dress. Mrs Fellowes asked the waiter to bring her a pair of scissors, and without interrupting the conversation, cut off the ostrich feathers from her black dress, and used them instead as a fan.

Isabella Blow
Oberto Gili, 1992

The real number of women who dress in a bizarre manner is, of course, much higher. There are duchesses who routinely dress like bag ladies, and bag ladies who dress like duchesses. There are women who, through some kink or impediment, let the world go by and continue to dress exactly the way that they did when they were children, or perhaps the way they did when they were happy and admired. They are recognized figures in their local communities, where they are taken for granted, which is what they like to be. These occasionally sad and lost women belong in the 'Miss Haversham' file, but pass almost unnoticed in the extraordinary variety of costume to be seen on any city street today. To be noted and acknowledged, the eccentric dresser of yesterday or today must have a high profile. Just like the conventional beauty, she has to be photographed and profiled and seen in the right places with the right people before she becomes a recognized phenomenon.

Both wars gave women extraordinary confidence, and the periods that followed – the 1920s and the 50s – were eras of extreme and exuberant fashion changes. Doing jobs, wearing trousers, practicing contraception, women stopped copying their mothers and dared to be themselves at last. But when an entire generation learns to dress in a more experimental way, how does a woman stand out from the crowd and get noticed? Upper-crust women pursued their usual goal of marriage to the wealthy and influential with a new appreciation of the help that could come from the society pages and fashion magazines. It had become an unspoken pact. The debutantes had to get themselves noticed before the press would take an interest. After that, the media obliged by building them up as characters for the entertainment of the public. One of the cleverest debs was Margaret Whigham, dark and sharp of feature, who learnt to play the press game so well that she held regular press conferences, ultimately snaring the Duke of Argyll.

The third and youngest daughter of the Duke of Rutland grew up at the end of the war, determined to make her mark. It wasn't enough that she was angelically blonde and beautiful and lived in Belvoir Castle, but it helped. Her mother brought her up along highly unusual aesthetic lines. As a child she was always dressed in black velvet, and as a debutante she wore grey and beige instead of the usual white and pink. It is easy to make yourself conspicuous if you know what everyone else will be wearing. Choosing the opposite became her theme. At Ascot she was easy to pick out among all the pastel straw hats in a black picture hat with sheaves of gold and silver wheat wrapped around the brim. When she joined with a group of society daughters dressed as swans for one of the pageants that were laid on for house party entertainment in the 20s, a ripple of irritation must have been noticeable from

Diana Vreeland
Horst P. Horst, 1979

the other debutantes as she appeared as the only black swan. She was to become Lady Diana Cooper, soon to be described in the press as 'the loveliest young Englishwoman of her generation'. Admired and envied for three generations, she was too worldly, and perhaps too pretty, to continue as an eccentric dresser. Instead she came to dress in whatever was the best and most flattering in fashion, her changes of appearance reflecting the course of fashion since 1919.

It is often mothers who, one way or another, set their daughters' course to E for eccentric. Baba d'Erlanger's, like Diana Cooper's, had brought her up to be highly unusual. As a child she was accompanied by a robed and turbanned mameluke, who followed her about like a slave, a mixture of nanny and bodyguard. The d'Erlangers lived in Byron's old house in Piccadilly, and gave marvellous children's parties to which Baba always wore gold. A spoiled belle-laide with a monkey face and scarlet lipstick, she became the Princess de Faucigny Lucinge, and set a later fashion for dressing up for the beach, wearing her white bathing suits with a tarbush cap, diamonds and bunches of shiny artificial fruit.

All eccentric dressers have a strong character, or they would be too timid to brave the city pavements. Politically incorrect as it may be to say so, most of them are striking rather than beautiful, strong-featured rather than pretty. If these women feel themselves to be plain, or if their families are insensitive enough to make them feel so, they can react by pushing their appearance to the outer edge. Like the nonpareils of Beau Brummel's day, they simply make themselves incomparable. The most strangely dressed eccentric of her day, the celebrated poet Dame Edith Sitwell, had a father who from her earliest age made her feel that she was plain, and therefore insignificant.

One of her brothers, the writer Osbert Sitwell, described her as a young girl 'with her face of brooding and luminous melancholy, with her lank, green-gold hair, and her features, of so distinctive a kind, but which her character, though developing so fast, had not yet fully carved out of the soft matrix of childhood'. With her Plantagenet looks and the profile of a gothic effigy, she looked as she grew up like an etiolated medieval figure, who would have been at her best in a wimple. When she was a child, the whole family was painted by John Singer Sargent in the drawing room at the family house, Renishaw. Osbert noted: 'My father, who ... only admired in a female small du-Maurier-like features, pointed out to the painter that my sister's nose deviated slightly from the perpendicular, and hoped that he would emphasise this flaw ... Sargent showed plainly that he regarded this as no way in which to speak of her personal aspect in front of a very shy and supersensitive child of eleven. Perhaps, too, he may

already have divined in her face and physique the germ of a remarkable and distinguished appearance which was later to appeal particularly to painters. At any rate, he made her nose straight in his canvas and my father's nose crooked.'

She very cleverly made the most of her strange, ecclesiastical face and figure, dressing in long medieval robes, often with a large black hat or strange turban above her lank bobbed hair, and piling enormous rings on to the long fingers of her delicate hands. She could not be compared with any other woman of her day, and continued all her life to look like the intellectual abbess of a 15th-century convent.

Nancy Cunard, journalist and poet, was the model for the elusive, fascinating 20s fictional heroine, Iris Storm in The Green Hat, a popular romantic novel of the day by Michael Arlen. She was one of the most conspicuous, decadent figures of her day, and during the late 20s wrote for Vogue as a regular correspondent, reporting on jazz and other avant-garde art forms from Paris. She powdered her face dead white and outlined her eyes with kohl, balancing them with lips painted so dark that they were almost black. Her dark wavy hair was cropped as short as a man's, with two curls slicked forward over her temples. Her clothes were typical of the period, but she wore armfuls of African wooden bangles, and when she danced, or beat time to the music with her cigarette holder, she rattled.

Nancy was the daughter of Emerald Cunard, married to the famous shipping magnate, and a leading hostess. While her mother devoted herself to entertaining international society in her houses around the world, Nancy was left in England to endure a harsh educational and domestic regime until she should become old enough to be interesting. By that time, she had become a classic rebel. She determined to reject the establishment and spend her life in her own way, much of it devoted to irritating her mother. She published a book of poetry in 1922, and headed for bohemia in Paris. Before long, she discovered the perfect way of scandalising her mother, and society at large, by having a wild affair with the black jazz musician, Henry Crowther. Lady Cunard is said to have had the couple followed wherever they went, making sure that they were harassed and moved on wherever they chose to take refuge.

The life Nancy had chosen took its toll on her. Her famous rages and scenes were probably due to the drugs that she had learned to take among the musicians and artists who were her friends. She moved restlessly around the world until, an old lady, she was arrested for behaving in a drunk and disorderly fashion in the King's Road in 1960. The journalist Brigid Keenan tells the story of how at Nancy Cunard's court appearance, she

Dame Edith Sitwell
Cecil Beaton

Nancy Cunard
Man Ray, 1927

took off her shoes and threw them at the magistrate. She was certified insane and spent time in a mental institution. She was, in a way, the first hautbo, the first upper-crust beatnik, some 30 years before they came into existence.

The 1920s and even the 30s were not the era of the serene classic beauty or the fluffy blonde. The effect on women of the First World War was much greater than that of the Second World War, bringing them contraception, short skirts, flexible underwear, men's clothing and sports clothes. Celebrities with striking looks were, for the first time, more highly prized than pretty ones and included personalities from every part of society: Wallis Simpson, Coco Chanel, Virginia Woolf, Tallulah Bankhead, Margot Asquith, Schiaparelli and Suzanne Lenglen. Looking back on those days, Osbert Sitwell wrote 'Never before had the ugly woman enjoyed such a run for her ugliness as in these days, and after the war, the uglier, the more "amusing" her appearance was deemed to be; so that the "great beauty" ... stood almost at a disadvantage.'

The hostess, Lady Ottoline Morrell, had a profile that could slice butter. Her mass of chestnut hair framed a Byzantine face with black eyes and an extraordinarily long, sharp nose: she dressed in magnificent wide skirts of brocade and silk, and looked something like the Spanish Infanta as painted by Velasquez. Most of the great writers and poets of her day passed through the salon of her country house, Garsington, or visited her for tea at the apartment she kept at Garland's Hotel in Suffolk Street, London. In the country, such celebrities as the writers D.H. Lawrence and Lytton Strachey, the mathematician Lord Russell, and the economist Maynard Keynes could be found digging in the potato patch of her Arcadian colony, watched by Virginia Woolf and Vanessa Bell, or dressing up to perform charades or a dance after dinner.

The wider parameters of style were accepted by a public that had become visually more sophisticated. It was one consolation for the Russian Revolution that it had left half the Imperial Ballet exiled abroad. Decoration was in the air, and in apartments all over Paris, and a year or two later in London, chairs and lamp shades, cushions and tablecloths reflected the Grecian or Oriental visions of Bakst and Benois. The exotic beauty of the costumes and settings, the dancing of Karsavina, Lopokova, Pavlova, Rubinstein, Nijinsky, Massine and the music of Rimsky-Korsakov, Balakirev, Debussy and Tchaikovsky combined in the most majestic and romantic of escapist fantasies. The barbaric beauty of the new ballerinas, with their serpentine bodies and flashing black eyes, presented a new kind of ideal a million miles away from the blue-eyed blondes of the musical comedy stage.

Tallulah Bankhead
Cecil Beaton

For an entire decade, every fashion designer took some inspiration from the ballet, with dresses of metal bead embroidery, headdresses of shooting feathers, earrings dropping to the chest and sparkling Turkish trousers. The Decorative Arts Exhibition in Paris in 1925 took over where the Russians had left off, with its new geometry, rich colors, and its shapes and patterns from Cubism, the Bauhaus and Aztec Art. The clothes that resulted were modern and streamlined and functional, more masculine, and suited sporty, angular women with cropped hair who flew planes and drove cars.

The most remarkable of all the exotics of the 1920s was the black dancer Josephine Baker. The 'Original' Dixieland Jazz Band, composed of white musicians, had opened at the Hammersmith Palais as early as 1919, and there had been a lot of diluted jazz since, but in 1925 the real thing was seen and heard in Paris. It had already happened in New York, where socialites went into the fringes of Harlem to dance and watch, and Negroes, as they were called, were invited up to Park Avenue apartments to teach the Charleston and the Black Bottom. The first all-colored show – written, produced and acted by black artists – was Shuffle Along, to be seen on Broadway in 1923. Since then there had been Runnin' Wild, Chocolate Dandies, Honey, and Dover Street to Dixie.

The Revue Nègre was the first to come to France, where audiences were almost knocked out by the waves of energy and noise which engulfed them from the footlights. Josephine Baker in her frill of bananas became an overnight sensation. Nancy Cunard was ecstatic about the 'perfect delight ... of Josephine Baker, most astounding of mulatto dancers, in her necklets, bracelets, and flouncing feathered loincloths. The fuzz has been taken out of her hair, which shines like a dark blue crystal as she yodels ... and contorts her surprising form through a maze of complicated rhythms.' Another Vogue writer called her 'a woman possessed, a savage intoxicated with tom-toms, a shining machine, a danseur, an animal, all joint and no bones ... at one moment she is the fashion artist's model, at the next Picasso's'.

All of a sudden anything black was the rage: black and white décor, Babangi masks, heads wrapped in turbans, bracelets up the arm from elbow to shoulder, and all Negro dances, particularly the Charleston. A year or two later, when Baker had opened her own nightclub in Paris, John McMullin went to interview her. 'She has come in without a wrap, and the length of her graceful body, which is light sealskin brown, is swathed in a full blue tulle frock with a bodice of blue snakeskin ... she wears an enormous diamond ring and a very impressive diamond bracelet. Her hair, which naturally grows in tight curls, is plastered

JOSÉPHINE BAKER
Studio Keyston Talbot

close to her head with white of egg and looks as though it were painted on her head with black shellac. As she appears at the Folies Bergères, one is struck by her great decadence of line. When, for the finale, she wears only a diamante maillot of tulle and red gloves with diamond balls hanging from the tips of her fingers, the effect is up to the wildest imagination of Beardsley.' She went everywhere in her Voisin car, painted brown and upholstered in brown snakeskin exactly matched to her own skin, accompanied by a maid, a chauffeur, and a white esquimau dog bearing on top of its head the red imprint of her kiss.

In a sense, the Second World War put an end to this cavalcade of theatrical women, most of them European, who had reigned over Vogue's world for two decades and more. Life became too serious, and the involvement of the whole British population concentrated minds and hearts on the job in hand. The eccentricity was crushed out of fashion. The women we wanted to look like, even if they were originals at heart, were suddenly seen to be responsible, sensible, normal. Vogue went to the country to photograph Lady Diana Cooper in a headscarf and trousers, milking the cow on her farm, and Mrs John Betjeman running a vegetable garden and riding the dawn parachute patrol on the Berkshire downs.

Whereas the end of the First World War had brought emancipation and revolutionized women's dress, the reaction to wartime austerity in the late 1940s brought a longing for luxury. Never has haute couture been more powerful than it was during the 1950s, spearheaded by Christian Dior's 1947 New Look. It was a time when women really did buy Vogue to see what length of skirt to wear, season by season, and a time when a couturier's new collection was guarded against spies as if it were GCHQ. Everyone became a slave to fashion, and the new conformity had the effect of inhibiting any kind of grand individual statement in either dress or style.

Oddly, the exact opposite became true only a decade later. From the 1960s on, everyone was an exotic or an eccentric. There was no single way to dress any more, so no obvious way to be different. City streets, starting with London, became pageants where the young were all dressed to the nines in some sort of personal costume. On the King's Road, any Saturday, you could see art students in striped Madras cottons and boots, bandsman uniforms, flea market satins and velvets, tucked and pearl-buttoned Victorian underwear, crochet frocks, Afghan wedding dresses, and satin shirts with dewlap collars. By now, commercial fashion was alert to the bizarre as an essential source of inspiration – and on any of those Saturdays you might have also seen one of the Paris couturiers – it might be Yves Saint Laurent or Pierre Cardin – on the prowl among the public, looking for inspiration.

Josephine Baker
1933

Vivienne Westwood
Michael Roberts, 1987

Turning conventions inside out has become the stock-in-trade of designers. Just as Chanel invented 'poor chic', the eccentric Vivienne Westwood has expressed her aim as 'making the poor look rich and the rich look poor'. From a decade of épater la bourgeoisie in the King's Road, she opened the 1980s with the Pirates collection as worn by the pop group Adam and The Ants. Its tidal effect on the fashion world sold the look right across the age barriers. She went from dressing a street to dressing the world in a single move.

Her shop at 430 King's Road changed its name from Let It Rock to Too Fast to Live, Too Young to Die, then to Sex and Seditionaries and World's End as Westwood produced a stream of clothes unlike anything the fashion world had seen before. She picked through time and space and the 'untouchable' areas of big city life to give us rubberwear, bondage trousers, 'muscle' T-shirts from gay gyms, the ripped T-shirt, the triple-tongued sneaker graffiti prints, duster shoes, bras worn over dresses and shorts with pockets hanging on the outside, coronation crowns and the Cambridge rapist T-shirt, and she wore it all herself. The daughter of a cotton mill worker from Tintwistle, Manchester, she owed an enormous debt to pop promoter Malcolm McLaren, the father of one of her sons, for getting the world to listen, but she has moved on with a cornucopia of fashion images. As she says 'I'm overprogrammed with ideas.'

No beauty, she looks in fact like a provincial woman who might run a teashop or set up a stall selling bric-a-brac. Bypassing chic, she presents her ideas raw, on her own body – even the jewelled codpieces and tights that were perhaps her strangest costume. She has been voted by Women's Wear Daily 'one of the six most influential designers in the world'.

Today, a strong sense of unconventional style usually leads directly to a commercial post in the design or magazine world, or – for the few with a high degree of social clout – to the job of muse to a famous couturier. Eccentricity is a caged bird, embedded within the international conglomerate that is the fashion industry today, displayed first in the spectaculars that have replaced fashion shows and then sold in shops around the world.

Just as high fashion has undoubtedly gained by admitting Vivienne Westwood to their ranks, street fashion has lost out. Bizarre dressing is easy: it's in the shops, and money will buy it. Strange clothes are everywhere, but it is harder to be truly original than ever before. As the model Lauren Hutton once put it 'Fashion is what you're offered. Style is what you choose.' The great eccentrics here, if they were alive today, would have found it hard to detect the difference.

9 *waifs*

From time to time there is an emotional movement towards a certain type of woman. She is a kind of résumé of all our current street idols, most of them from the world of rock and other music, and she gradually comes to be recognized as the look of the moment.

In the 60s and again in the 90s, following decades in which high fashion dictates were followed to the letter, a new ideal emerged. Centered on individuality and a refusal to capitulate to the pressure to be perfect, the look was a step ahead of couture. In both decades, high fashion itself became unfashionable, and the signs were evident in the magazines.

In the 60s, the young owned the town, and the town they owned was primarily London. The new aristocracy, as they were called, included pop singers, photographers, actors and model girls, pop artists, hairdressers, interior decorators, writers and designers. The 15–19 year olds who had been a tiny fraction of the buying market in the mid-50s grew in number until, by 1967, they were buying about half of all the clothes being sold in the country. These young women tended to look and dress in a completely different way from their mothers, their immaturity emphasised by tiny skirts and boys' clothes, wide eyes staring from blackened eyelids that tangled with fringes as long as a Shetland pony's.

The new ideal was epitomized in the girlfriends of The Beatles, Jane Asher and Patti Boyd, the actresses Rita Tushingham, Julie Christie and Mia Farrow, the model phenomenon that was Jean Shrimpton, and the schoolgirl model Twiggy, with her knee socks and hair cut like a prep school boy's. For a while these child-women were coralled in Vogue in a sub-section called 'Young Idea', but by the mid 60s they filled the magazine. Created as a symbol of the revolution against high fashion and the ideas of the previous generation, the waif was quickly copied and co-opted by the couture.

By contrast, the recognition of the 90s waif, and her admission to Vogue at the beginning of the decade, was fashion's first, knee-jerk reaction to a drop in clothes sales. For several years, all the glamour of the fashion industry had been concentrated on the supermodels. From Paris to Papua New Guinea, just a handful of faces passed for perfection. Thousands of billions of dollars came to ride on the common determination that these women were the most beautiful and fashionable in the world. It was a conspiracy bent on harnessing them to purely commercial ends.

While the presence of these women on the catwalk ensured that the fashion shows caught the attention of the press, the designers and magazines had handed over the power to five or six stars and their increasingly demanding agents. Not only did these stars

Jane Asher
David Bailey, 1964

right:
Twiggy
Cecil Beaton, 1967

demand, and get, fees of up to $40,000 for one catwalk appearance, but more importantly, the models had become more important than the clothes. There was little or no direction to fashion any more, and all that counted was that the clothes shopper made the connection between the supermodel and the name on the label.

The introduction of the new waifs, by way of Seattle, grunge music and the ethos of Kurt Cobain, brought about a bizarre and short-lived subtext to the pages of Vogue. In reaction to the too-perfect look of women in the 80s, these women looked 'real', they were very young, and they stopped the reader in her tracks.

Over a couple of seasons models went from over- to under-whelming, and the magazines filled with pictures of Les Misérables knocking about in too-large frocks with rubber flip-flops, looking like refugees from the Dustbowl. Like Cinderella returned to the scullery, like graphs of the economy, the model image deflated. Skeletal, round-shouldered and oomphless, the waif, as photographed by David Sims, Paolo Roversi and art-photographers Nan Goldin and Richard Prince, looked too young, druggy and harmless to wield any power.

'We're now looking for the female equivalent of Jarvis Cocker,' British Vogue beauty director Polly Sellar told me in 1997. 'It takes a real, raw, weird face to catch a reader's attention. Look at the Jil Sander, Prada and Calvin Klein campaigns and you'll recognize the look – it's anyone and everyone, take-me-as-you-find-me, however pale and scrawny and greasy-haired.' One of the most influential of the subversive new photographers was Corinne Day, whose pictures of a 15-year old Kate Moss for The Face shot the waif-model to stardom. Day's world, showing ill-looking models in grungy vests and dingy flats, gave rise to the phrase 'heroin chic'.

The jolie-laides models led by Karl Lagerfeld's sometime muse Stella Tennant, and Iris Palmer, Esther de Jong and Guinevere Van Seenus, with the young Kate Moss by far the most prominent name, projected street attitude, independence and a rather magnificent individuality far from sex appeal. They glowered, stormed and frowned into the lens. The way they deliberately refused to glamorize themselves betrayed their determination not to be fashion victims. They might not have looked like the commodities of the fashion industry, but designers were soon using them to stake out their hip credentials, in order to capture a new generation not over eager to be labelled as biddable consumers.

Compare Kate Moss in her original and current incarnations, and you will see the difference. There was a raw forcefulness about her that made her look quirky, weird

Marianne Faithfull
David Bailey, 1965

following pages, left:
Penelope Tree
David Bailey, 1967
following pages, right:
Mia Farrow
David Bailey, 1965

right:
Kate Moss
Corinne Day, 1993

previous pages, left:
Esther de Jong
Robert Erdmann, 1996
previous pages,right:
Stella Tennant
Arthur Elgort, 1996

and almost intimidating. She used to scowl, and still looks as if she has a life of her own, remote from fashion. Today she is far more glamorous, but she still has none of that superior, alienatingly 'perfect' look of the supermodels. The grittiness of her appeal won her one of the top perfume campaigns of the 90s, Calvin Klein's CKOne advertising spreads, in which she dominates a line-up of youngsters who could be found on the streets of any provincial town. She is still the best-known model to have bridged the gap between waif and fashionista.

Vogue recorded the existence of the fashion waif through the work of photographers with MTV credentials, in the form of respected music videos. The magazine was as eager as the couturiers to attract the young. At the same time the magazine found ways to express its reservations. Men scoffed. 'I've never understood ... why beautiful women would want to look like heroin addicts who haven't washed their hair in two weeks', wrote one Vogue commentator, Christopher Buckley. 'The waif look was not a winner', sniffed New York socialite Blaine Trump. 'Oddly enough, combat boots do not do it for me.'

The repercussions of the two extremes, the supermodel and the waif, are with us yet. Clothes are still pretty insignificant. For a while you have hardly been meant to notice them, except as frames for great legs and hollow midriffs. But, in the end, power always returns to the money, and the money, here, comes from an industry whose only constant is that it continually changes. Much has been said about women as victims of the fashion and beauty industries, with anorexia presumed to be caused by the example of skeletal models, and children of 14 stalking the catwalks.

But nothing in fashion is compulsory. Women buy, or they don't buy. And on this one, they voted with their feet. For the time being, at least, fashion is regaining its balance.

10 *icons*

Icons, as opposed to stars, and even superstars, are remembered beyond the century and live lives of Shakespearean drama and sometimes of historic significance. Subsection Vogue Women narrows the category even further to women of great beauty and high profile. Cleopatra would count as a Vogue icon: Mrs Thatcher never did, nor did Mother Teresa.

You can find out everything about a starlet, down to the color of her bedroom, but we can never know enough about icons to satisfy our curiosity. How could Jackie Kennedy marry Onassis? Come to that, how could she marry into the Kennedys? How did she cope, living with Jack? What would Diana have done next? Marry Dodie? Go to America? How did Monroe die? Was it because she had been the lover of Jack and Bobbie, and she was beginning to talk? What gave Liz Taylor the right to so many husbands and so many diamonds? Why did Garbo want to be alone?

A star changes course at her peril, and yet cannot rest on her laurels. An icon, as Elizabeth Taylor once said, can do what she damn well likes. The public are so obsessed that they will follow their idols through a lifetime of reverses and metamorphoses. We love triumph. We like to back a winner. Garbo wouldn't have been an icon had she lived today, because she didn't let us into her life. Diana and Elizabeth Taylor did, Jackie Kennedy and Monroe had no choice.

The world changes around these people, and when they age it is as if an entire era has aged with them. 'Liz Taylor is 40!' is all Life magazine needed to say on the cover of their 25 February 1972 issue. 'When Elizabeth Taylor becomes 40 years old this week', wrote journalist Thomas Thompson, 'the sea will not boil, nor will the earth convulse and crack ... but there will certainly be the feeling that all of us are suddenly middle-aged.' At the age of 68, Elizabeth Taylor is in London to celebrate an exhibition dedicated to her at the National Portrait Gallery and to be created a Dame of the British Empire at Buckingham Palace. Seven marriages – two of them to Richard Burton – and countless different ailments have not impaired her sparkle. Of all 20th-century Vogue icons, she is and always has been the best suited to the role. She became a legend, then outlived it. Each and every detail of her life still fascinates.

This was a woman who ordered take-aways from other continents. Chilli con carne from Chasen's in LA followed her daily to Rome; English traditional pork sausages from Fortnum & Mason pursued her to Leningrad. On nights before she traveled, a British Airways executive would camp out in her drawing room to ensure she didn't miss her flight – for, as Richard Burton said, she would be late for the Last Judgement.

THE ELIZABETHANS AT HOME

Elizabeth Taylor
Henry Clarke, 1967

The Helen of Troy de nos jours, she has mauve moonstone eyes with, unusually, natural double rows of long black eyelashes. Her skin is white, her spiky, short hair is black. She is 5 feet 6 inches tall. I met her in the $3 million house that spreads itself over 10,000 square feet of Bel Air. The famous face and teased hair lifted proudly out of the Hamlet collar of a cream silk shirt. Round hips were jazzily belted over tight black jeans. Bracelets chinked, earrings winked, brassy things jingled, clouds of scent wafted around her. Her whole presence was endearingly, ridiculously feminine. She was just about to marry for the seventh time, to a bubble-curled ex trucker, and she told me in her breathy, baby voice that she couldn't remember a time that she wasn't famous.

At 18, courtesy of her first husband, Nicky Hilton, she had stocks, minks, a Cadillac convertible, and a ring worth $50,000. At 24, courtesy of Mike Todd, she had a cinema named after her, a present every day – and a big one on Saturdays 'cos that's the day they met – a Rolls, a 30-carat diamond measuring an inch and a half across, and paintings by Degas and Vuillard. At 31, courtesy of Richard Burton and Twentieth Century-Fox, she earned a million dollars a picture, owned the Krupp diamond – 'Thirty-three and a third carats, and don't forget the third!' she counselled me – Shah Jehan's pale yellow diamond that candlelight showed was carved with words of love, the Peregrina pearl owned by Mary Tudor in 1554, houses in Mexico and Gstaad, the penthouse at the Dorchester in London, and a yacht. 'Richard was generous,' she said. 'And not to a fault. To a glorious degree!'

Smart as paint under the sensual silken manner, witty and wise, she chose to come across as an arch vulgarian. She was actually an upper-crust girl who grew up with a weekend home in the English countryside, a pony, paintings by Augustus John on the walls and dance lessons at Madame Vacani's, where that other Elizabeth, the Queen, went too. She evacuated with her family from Britain to Hollywood during the war, and became a child star in such films as Lassie Come Home and National Velvet, the box-office hit about a girl and a racehorse. By the time she was 12 she was on her fifth film, earning $300 a week, and entrancing the press. Asked 'Do you think you're already a film star?' she shot back, 'All those men taking their daughters to National Velvet – do you think they were looking at the horse?'

When she became pregnant for the first time, in Hollywood, and had to beg for a loan and time off, she was humiliated and exploited. It was never allowed to happen again. She was to develop a steeliness which has brought whole studios to their knees.

She was posing for cheese-cake photographs when she was 15, and by her early 30s she and Richard Burton were the world's most famous couple and could guarantee spectacular audience figures for any movie they were in. Even so, the failed blockbuster Cleopatra nearly sank Twentieth Century-Fox. To break even, the movie had to bring in over $40 million.

The Cleopatra fiasco damaged her reputation for a moment. A new generation tried to remember: could someone that beautiful really act? She answered the question in 1969 with Who's Afraid of Virginia Woolf?, with a shattering performance in which beauty had no part.

At heart, she is an earth mother. She has three children – Liza, Christopher and Michael – and adopted a fourth, Maria, a crippled German child soon transformed by remedial surgery. Elizabeth Taylor was a world-famous worker for charity before Princess Diana was ten years old, giving millions to children's causes, and the air around her Bel Air house was filled with a cacophony of cackling, bleating and barking from the countless animals she has rescued along the way. Her entourage at the height of her fame consisted of the four children and two nannies, five dogs, two secretaries, one budgerigar, one chauffeur, one wildcat, one hairstylist, one valet, one dressmaker, one turtle that had to be kept in water, and 140 pieces of luggage.

She was a survivor, a full-blooded lover and liver who said of her explosive marriage to Mike Todd, 'We had more fun fighting than most people have making love.' She was no feminist: she was too feminine. 'I don't think you have to burn bras,' she told me in her small voice. 'I like bras, and I love lace underwear!'

She told me that she thought the most beautiful woman in the world was Audrey Hepburn. 'But the way I look is all right with me.' 'I don't entirely approve of some of the things I have done, or am, or have been,' she told me. 'But I'm me. God knows, I'm me.' And at the end of the interview, she quoted her favourite poem, 'The Leaden Echo and The Golden Echo', by Gerald Manley Hopkins:

How to keep – is there any any, is there none such, nowhere known some,
bow or brooch or braid or brace, lace, latch or catch or key to keep
Back beauty, keep it, beauty, beauty, beauty, ... from vanishing away?

While Liz Taylor was born for the spotlight, Diana had to learn. She learnt so well that she became a genius at communicating her emotions, even when officially voiceless, and she enslaved the hearts of the nation. Through her image in print and on

Diana
Patrick Demarchelier, 1997

screen, she was able to edit and express the story of her life for a worldwide audience, and never needed an interpreter. When she underwent the metamorphosis from superstar to icon, at the time of the royal divorce – and in an echo of Elizabeth Taylor's 'I'm me' – Diana said 'From now on, I am going to own myself and be true to myself. I no longer want to live someone else's idea of what and who I should be.'

She came to fame as a Princess, but Diana's own appeal proved much stronger. The wonder was that a royal woman who had everything, a woman with beauty, children, money, and the world at her feet, could go through what so many of us go through. She, too, agonized over a painful marriage, separation and divorce, a sense of being worthless, the terrible fear that we have failed our children and are losing them, and psychological trauma. She emerged as a legend for a modern woman, independent and finally triumphant.

Diana had wondered whether she would be remembered as the Marilyn Monroe or Jackie Kennedy of her day. As she learned to stand on her own and transcend her fashion image, her fame and mystique matched theirs. The pundits who had predicted that the 'electric charge' between the Princess and the public would dissipate when she was divorced were proved wrong. Losing her royal title only concentrated attention on her as a martyr, sacrificed to a dysfunctional royal family. Public affection erected a dome of protection around her, so that even the combined forces of the House of Lords, the Church of England, academia and the royalists could not denigrate her. She said, in so many words, 'I want to be a queen of people's hearts.' She had become a worldwide obsession, deeply rooted in the human psyche – in other words, an icon.

Four thousand people filed through the London auction rooms to view the clothes she sold for charity. Five thousand more did the same in New York. Millions watched the auction on television, while the thousands who had camped out in the heatwave fought for a place from which they could see her go by. The auction raised $3,258,750, making her one of the world's great philanthropists. She no longer needed a royal title, as her brother was to say, to generate her particular brand of magic. What had a title or clothes to do with what Mother Teresa had taught her to call 'God's work on earth'? By the time she was given the Humanitarian of the Year Award in December 1996, and Dr Henry Kissinger had praised the way she had 'aligned herself with the ill, the suffering and the downtrodden', her mystique had reached its peak. The power of an icon is formidable. The shy kindergarten teacher and home help had developed into a personality who had changed the monarchy, softened the mood of the country, and even influenced in a small way the political priorities of the world.

The precious icons of the Greek Orthodox Church were supposed, in themselves, to confer blessings, and take on the properties of saints. Diana the symbol, sanctified by sudden early death, underwent a temporary further transformation. Filing through the Palace of St James to add their names to the tribute books, several people in the queue thought they saw her face in an old painting. Some tourists at Kensington Palace swore they saw her looking down on them from a high window. There are still people who burn a candle for her in a home-made shrine decorated with pages torn out of magazines and newspapers.

If there was one world figure with whom Diana really did compare herself, and studied and copied, it was Jackie Kennedy. Jackie had a significance for Diana that came from many similarities. Jackie had been as stylish, charismatic, admired and emulated as Diana, and her life was as full as Diana's of world-shaking crises and astonishing, even horrifying developments. Like Diana, Jackie had centered her world on her children, and she was terrified of losing them to the powerful family she had married into. Like Diana, she had spent fortunes on her clothes and was given fabulous jewels. Like Diana, Jackie had been called the greatest single fashion influence in modern history. For Diana, as for Jackie during her years as First Lady, clothes were a vital aid to representing your country, and virtually the only way of communicating with your public.

In photographs of Jackie Kennedy one can see the source of so many of Diana's trademark dresses. When the Princess met the Pope in 1985, she played it safe, just as Jackie had when she visited Pope John XXIII in 1962, by wearing a full-length black dress with a veil. And then there were the one-shouldered evening gowns, the sparkling embroideries, the slender columns of white lace, the bell-shaped skirts of duchesse satin gathered in a bow at the princess-line bodice, the fluid white Grecian drapes, the pale, sleeveless sheath dresses and the pillbox hats.

Oleg Cassini, who designed the First Lady's wardrobe during the thousand days of the Kennedy administration, had invented the pillbox to sit on the back of the head and not disarrange the thick, bouffant fringe. 'The pillbox is a non-hat,' explained Cassini. 'The focus should be on the face.' Diana's milliner, Philip Somerville, told me that the Princess liked to wear her hats the same way, on the back of her head so as not to flatten her fringe. That was the moment she asked him if he thought that one day she would be thought of as the Jackie Kennedy of her day. On her Washington visit, Diana was hailed as precisely that – the new Jackie Kennedy, more royal than the royals.

Like so many stars, Jackie Kennedy was groomed for success by a pushy mother. The nouveau riche Janet Lee Bouvier, mother of Jackie and Lee, moved for a quickie divorce from their father, 'Black' Jack Bouvier, with his womanizing and $64,000 of debts, and set her cap at the vast fortune of Hugh Auchincloss. An investment banker who had inherited Standard Oil money, Auchincloss headed New York society with family connections linking him to the Vanderbilts, Rockefellers, du Ponts, Tiffanys and Saltonstalls. When Janet had become Mrs Auchincloss, there was the 46 acre Merrywood estate in Virginia and the 75 acre Hammersmith Farm in Newport, each with its fleet of Rolls Royces, its stables and tennis courts, butlers, housekeepers and maids. Jackie had a few boyfriends, but her mother succeeded in laughing any engagement out of court until the appearance of Jack Kennedy.

The Kennedy wedding went down in American history. By special arrangement with the Vatican, bride and groom received the Apostolic Blessing of Pope Pius XII, and 1200 guests attended the wedding. Three thousand spectators gathered outside the gates to glimpse the bride, and saw more of her than her inebriated father, who was deftly manoeuvred out of the celebrations by Mrs Auchincloss.

From that moment, Jackie was sacrificed to the political ambitions and ends of the Kennedys. It seems very likely that at some stage Joe Kennedy both threatened and bribed her to remain in a marriage she detested. Jack Kennedy's womanizing would have been enough to poison the marriage, but she was expected to have a large family despite the difficulty she had with childbirth. Three of her pregnancies ended in deaths. Her four caesareans and many miscarriages left her with an acute anxiety about the health and safety of her son and daughter.

She was, perhaps, the most cultivated First Lady of the century. She spoke fluent French, and had once won the Vogue Talent Contest for an essay on Oscar Wilde, Charles Baudelaire and Serge Diaghilev. She enchanted Krushchev and Charles de Gaulle, and – like Diana – had ended by eclipsing her husband on shared trips abroad. She instigated the restoration of the White House as a national treasure. Her nationally televised tour of the building, expounding in her little-girl voice on the remarkable furniture and pictures, captivated and impressed 50 million Americans. As Women's Wear Daily was to put it years later, she did more in that one afternoon to uplift taste levels in the United States than any other woman in its history.

The assassination in Dallas altered her. As if in a dream, she clambered over the presidential car, trying to collect together her husband's shattered head. Nobody will

Jackie Kennedy
Marilyn Silverstone, 1962

forget, either, the moment when she stepped off the plane at Andrews Air Force Base on the night of 22 November 1963, with her husband's blood on the skirt of her pale pink Chanel suit. Friends and family feared she would lose her mind altogether. She could not bring herself to tell her children of their father's death, and their nurse had to do it for her. Her speech became slurred, and her eyes were sunken and dead. She lost interest in her appearance and crept around the house in a dirty dress, hair unwashed.

At Jack's funeral, veiled in thick black lace and standing by her children, the three-year-old saluting proudly at her knee, she achieved sainthood in the eyes of the public. To the trauma of a murdered husband, even before her marriage to Onassis, was added the murder of a brother-in-law. She could do no wrong until she married Aristotle, after which, as she used to say, she could do no right.

She met him on board his yacht, The Christina, in 1963. Her sister Lee Radziwill was there with the Roosevelts, and had suggested she join them to help her recover from the death of her latest baby, Patrick, who had died after only 39 hours of life. Listlessly, she did so, markedly unimpressed by Ari's manners, his yellow seaplane, the private cinema, the nine guest rooms, or the bar stools covered with skin from the testicles of whales. Then she had returned to the White House, to ready herself for the trip to Texas.

It seemed to the world that Jackie, after all, lived for money. As soon as she had signed the pre-nuptual agreement, Onassis settled $5 million on her, and presented her with a fortune in jewels. On her marriage she acquired a Greek island with 72 servants, apartments in all the European capitals that counted, and a privately owned airline. The newspapers called it 'The $20 million Honeymoon'. Every fortnight Ali sent her a bouquet in which was concealed either a bracelet or a necklace.

As if horrified by the marriage she had made, Jackie took him for everything he could provide, honoring only the bare legal terms of the nuptual contract. She went shopping crazy, trying to wound him through checkbook warfare. She would buy 36 pairs of shoes in a day, not even using her king's ransom of a dress allowance to pay for them, but charging them instead to Ari's Olympic Airlines. She would sell clothes the day after she bought them, and pocket the cash.

Was it for money she married the swarthy latter-day pirate, crude, untutored and aging? Was that the reason that she had tied up her future with that of a former telephone operator and tobacco importer who ate raw onions for breakfast, drank himself under the table nightly and loved to brag about his famous guests, who included Sir Winston

Churchill and Princess Grace, the Burtons and the great diva Maria Callas, his mistress? The best guess is that she married him for the security that only vast amounts of money can provide – and not for her own safety, but for that of her beloved John and Caroline. While the Secret Service already provided four men to tail the children around the clock, she perhaps needed to protect them from a danger closer at hand.

The rumor was that the Kennedys had plans for her and for John. Before his death, Bobbie was a constant visitor at her house, vetting her appearances in public, policing her private life to keep suitors at bay, taking decisions about the children's schooling. As far as he and the family were concerned, Jackie's role, now she was a public saint and icon, was to stand on political platforms alongside Bobby, bringing in the emotional vote, helping the Kennedys to stay on top of the world.

Her children were everything to her, and she was prepared to make who knows what sacrifices to keep them out of the family's hands. As soon as her children were safely grown, and as if to refute her reputation as a golddigger, she took a job as consulting editor of Viking Press for a salary of $10,000 a year, and disappeared into the woodwork of New York. Two years later she swapped jobs, but only to work for Doubleday in a similar role for slightly more money. Perhaps she regarded the really important part of her life as over – her role as mother. In one of her few recorded personal utterances, she memorably said 'If you bungle raising your children, I don't think whatever else you do matters very much.'

There was another icon who was running scared of the Kennedys. Marilyn Monroe, with her brimming figure, the perfect legs she revealed to the hilt in the famous skirt-blowing scene from The Seven Year Itch, and her heavy painted eyelids, was 'The Sex Goddess'. She was also the sometime mistress of Jack and Bobby, and she was indiscreet.

In the tradition of screen blondes, she had the friendly vulgarity of Jean Harlow, but she could parody sex appeal to the point of comedy. Her undulating walk, it was said, was caused by the weak ankles which wobbled on her six inch heels. Like Jackie Kennedy and Elizabeth Taylor, she spoke in a breathy, soft voice as if she were still a little girl. Of her pithy utterances, most people can only remember that she said she slept in three drops of Chanel Number 5. She didn't have to talk. She conveyed volumes with her eyes, her hips and her slight, vague gestures. In real life, she found it more and more difficult to make public appearances. It was as if the cinema realized her own dreams and fantasies to an extraordinary degree, and that her life on camera was more real, even to her, than her confused and lonely private life.

In her first important film at the age of 21, the sophisticated 1947 Bette Davis vehicle All About Eve, she made a short but devastating appearance as a party guest encountering her first butler. But her career didn't take off until 1952, and her last movie, The Misfits, was made only nine years later. In that short space of time, she had established a screen personality more voluptuous and zany than any of her contemporaries' and passed into history as the woman most men would like to bed.

The director Joshua Logan said 'Monroe is pure cinema. She is the most completely realized and authentic film actress since Garbo.' Privately, she was unstable and damaged by her upbringing. Lacking in confidence, she could never get herself together for her call to camera, and became a byword for keeping the crew waiting hour after hour while the director knocked at her trailer door and studio executives counted the cost of her contract. At Madison Square Garden, in May 1962, they announced her three times on stage before she appeared from the wings to celebrate the president's birthday. 'And here is the late Marilyn Monroe,' said Peter Lawford, as she shimmered on in a dress of skin-coloured chiffon that left her looking almost naked, to sing 'Happy birthday, Mr President' in a bedroom voice that sent the audience crazy. Then John Kennedy stepped forward to pay his own respects: 'I can now retire from politics, after having "Happy Birthday" sung to me by Miss Monroe.' It was an extraordinary moment, given the subtext of their lives. Less than three months later, after pestering the president's office with scores of desperate phone calls, the movie icon was dead.

Monroe and Garbo, the daughter of a Swedish labourer, both attained icon status through the lives they lived on screen. Neither of them, perhaps, could believe what had happened to them, and both were terrified that if they appeared without the lighting, the make-up, the clothes and the support of the technical wizards, the magic would break and the mirror would crack from side to side.

Greta Garbo had been the lather girl in a barber's shop when she began to play extras in Swedish films. Her extreme shyness was at odds with her screen image, and together with her foreign accent gave her the reputation in Hollywood for being formal and haughty. Her relationship with MGM was one of icy formality, so much so that Howard Strickling, the head of the publicity department, had her enigmatic face pasted on to a photograph of the Sphinx at Gaza. On screen, her haunting beauty overwhelmed the audience, with her lank vanilla hair, deep-set gentian blue eyes and lashes so long they cast shadows on her cheekbones. Whereas she had once rubbed her face in Scandinavian snow, in Hollywood she began each day by rubbing her skin with ice cubes.

Marilyn Monroe
Eve Arnold, 1960

She bridged the gap between the early movies and the talkies, and usually played a broken blossom, a vulnerable creature with an erotic atmosphere, sacrificing herself for love. She was perhaps best known in Hollywood to Adrian, the costume designer, who said that she always 'brought to the sets, with her quality of aloofness, that mystery which is part of her and part of the theatre's integral glamor'.

When her first talkie, Eugene O'Neill's Anna Christie, was released in 1930, her army of fans sat on the edge of their seats. It had been said that her voice was gutteral and thickly Swedish. They were disarmed and enchanted with her first words, 'Gif me a viskey, chincher ale on the side – and don't be stingy, baby.' When her shoulder-length pageboy and slouch hat began to be universally copied, it signalled the end of the 20s.

Adrian excelled himself for Garbo. When she starred in a movie biography of Queen Christina of Sweden, whose throne by tradition could only be inherited by males, Adrian exploited her flat chest and wide shoulders, together with her somewhat ambiguous erotic quality, by turning her into a gloriously dashing cavalier. She wore high, starched white collars framing her face, military jackets, padded shoulders and thigh boots. Christina, stifled by a life of formality and ceremony, with a masculine education and a modern, complicated sexuality, suited Garbo perfectly and confirmed her status as a unique cinema idol.

The true test of an icon is longevity. Even after their death, you go on and on seeing photographs of them, and being interested in their life and style. In the West, icons are understood to exert a good influence, and to spend at least a proportion of their time and money in helping the less fortunate. It is different in African countries, and in the Far East, where people vote for patronage and privilege, and for female icons rich and powerful enough to hold over them an umbrella of protection. The Eva Perons and Imelda Marcoses of this world are names to conjure with, the Peronistas still a political party standing for the rights of the poor against landowning and big business, Madame Marcos threatening to return on an unexpected wave of popularity. In the West we prefer our icons to be sensitive to our needs by virtue of suffering. We like them to triumph, but not to grow too different from ourselves.

Who might be our next icon? Perhaps a virtuous symbol of motherhood, faithful to her man, whose life will predictably suffer some severe setbacks ... perhaps staunch, beautiful, popular Jemima Khan, trapped by love and marriage in a country that has persecuted her for her husband's politics. In a world of copies, she is still, as of the millennium, the real thing.

Greta Garbo
Cecil Beaton, 1946

acknowledgements

My grateful thanks go to the following:

Colin Webb and Vivien James of Pavilion and my editor there, Morwenna Wallis; Alexandra Shulman and Nicolas Coleridge at Condé Nast, and Lisa Hodgkins in the library; Andrea Whittaker, who located the pictures and Mark Thomson who designed the book; Robert Morgan, Editor of The Sunday Times Magazine; Christopher Bailey and Gwen Howell ... and the cavalcade of Vogue Women, past and present, to whom this book is dedicated.

index

Page numbers in italics refer to illustrations.

credits

Other pictures by kind permission of the following:
Associated Press 49
Cecil Beaton photographs courtesy of Sotheby's Picture Library, London 28, 29, 31, 114, 143, 175
Camera Press 7, 14, 16, 18, 19, 20, 22, 41, 76, 101, 122, 125, 128
William Claxton 99
Express Newspapers 32
Horst/Hamilton's/Fiona Cowan 138
Hulton Getty 38, 39, 40, 96, 110, 144
The Illustrated London News Picture Library 15, 30
Magnum 168, 172
Norman Parkinson Ltd/Fiona Cowan 46, 47, 75, 78, 79, 88, 92, 95